Fresh Fire that woke the Remnant of Christ

Mark Ray Wilson

ISBN: 0692338322
ISBN 13 9780692338322

Contents

Introduction

The Year Was 2014

"Who Are the Remnants?"

"By night on my bed I sought him whom my soul loves. I sought him but I found him not. I will arise now and will go about the city, in the streets and in the broad ways I will seek him whom my soul loves; I sought him but I found him not. The watchman that goes about the city found me; to whom I said, "'Have you seen the one to whom my soul loves?' It was a little while after I passed them that I found him whom my soul loves; I held him and I would not let him go, until I brought him into my mother's house, and into the chamber of her that conceived me" (Song of Sol. 3:1–4).

The remnants of Christ love the Lord and desire to be in His presence. Wherever His name is mentioned, in a public or private setting, they smile and are very interested in what is being said. The remnants want and seek His presence and will drive miles and go to great lengths to be with Him. They dress for Him, and they think about Him with a passion. They meditate on the things He said and is saying. They want an intimate relationship with Him. Intimate can be read as "in-to-me-see." The remnants want to please Him and want their lamps to be full of the oil of the Holy Spirit. The remnants are constantly looking for His appearing and long for the day that they can be with Him whom their souls love.

one

The Times, They Are a-Changin'

There is growing trouble on the planet lately. It almost seems like Mother Nature has turned against us. Isaiah 24:20 says the earth shall stagger like a drunken man and shall sway to and fro like a hammock, its transgressions weighing heavily upon it, and it shall fall and not rise again. Man's knowledge has increased so that there are claims of weather modifications through transmitters that alter and bombard the ionosphere with low frequency transmissions, causing the same scenarios as a solar flare. Hundreds of airplanes are leaving chemical trails in a checkerboard pattern across the sky, dropping aluminum-based reflective material that increases the efficiency of the device. The weapon was developed to modify weather patterns, disrupt communications, and stop missile-guidance systems. It was created during President Reagan's term. They called it the Star Wars system. The program was suddenly squelched when the US Army and Navy bought this weapons patent from a man named Dr. Eastland. We thought the Star Wars had been stopped only to discover that a weapon had been created capable of altering weather, causing an electromagnetic pulse, heating up regions, or destroying missiles anywhere on the planet. The chaos and damage it has done to the planet's delicate ecosystem may never be repaired. Mankind has gotten too smart and now has an ego unparalleled since the Tower of Babel.

"Lift up your eyes to the heavens and look upon the earth beneath; for the heavens shall be dissolved and vanish away like smoke, and the earth shall wax old like a garment (get holes in its covering) and they that dwell therein shall die in like manner, like gnats, but my salvation shall be forever, and my rightness and judgment (and faithfully fulfilled promise) shall not be abolished" (Isa. 51:6).

Talk of a new world order and one world government is in the news nearly every day. However, that is not as shocking as the execution of a one-world religion. It is unthinkable to me. Social media and the world are challenging everything the believer in Jesus Christ stands for. We are called haters for the stands that we take against sin in any form. I guess we represent judgment to them when the fact is we do not have the power to judge anyone. A person's actions and decisions will matter on judgment day. God wrote the laws, and Jesus brought us grace. But be not deceived that law and grace came from the same author, Lord, and judge. Jesus Christ and God are the only righteous judges that ever lived.

I long for the days of years gone by when right and wrong were more defined and agreed on because the Bible was our guide to life here on earth and in the hereafter. Sin wants to be applauded and is considered brave instead of rebellion. Sin has never been more socially accepted than it is right now.

It has attacked the core of Christianity. How long has it been since you heard a gospel message about the birth, life, death, or second coming of the Lord Jesus Christ? Some services are like pep rallies. We seem to have lost our anchor. An anchor on a ship will allow that ship to go a little to the left or right; however, it will not let the ship get way out there. Some churches have way out there and lost their anchor. We must get back to Jesus, our first love.

two

The Calling

She was awakened at four o'clock in the morning. That was not as strange as it may sound because it was the fourth watch of the night when visions and special words from the master were downloaded. Ellen is a prayer warrior, and this had happened so many times that she was not alarmed. She got up from her bed and began making her way to the screened-in back porch where she could sit in her familiar rocking chair to listen and pray. Her hands rubbed the worn wooden grooves that her mother's and dad's fingers had made as they sat in that same old rocking chair when they had a pressing need or trial. Ellen wondered what they were praying about when they sat in that chair.

The August night was balmy and made her skin feel clammy. The smell of freshly cut hay was in the air. Ellen was alive with anticipation to hear what the Holy Spirit had to say. She loved the Lord with all her heart and longed to hear His voice, not through the mind of her spirit as now but in person. Ellen leaned back in her favorite chair and pondered how good the Lord had been to her. Even though she had seen the events of the times, she knew she was a child of God and she was going to be all right.

Ellen closed her eyes and began to repeat Jesus's name. As she opened the eyes of her spirit in prayer, the trees outside her home seemed to sway to the left and right as they began to think about their creator. Their limbs stretched upward toward the Lord Jesus as a form of praise. because in this dimension nothing else matters, and because He is still the talk of heaven. It has always been about Jesus.

Ellen found herself in a large expanse where worship was taking place. She saw creatures that were made to worship all the time. The light in this dimension emanated from the Father—the purest white she had ever seen. His glory was the light source of heaven.

She saw a four-footed beast covered with eyes, walking back and forth across the throne room, crying, "Holy, holy, holy."

"And I saw four living creatures, individually having six wings, were full of eyes all over, even underneath their wings, and day or night they never stopped saying 'Holy, holy, holy is the Lord God Almighty omnipotent, who was and is and is to come'" (Rev. 4:8, AMP).

Angels came up and down as the prayers of the saints were executed. "Jacob dreamed, and behold, there was a ladder set up on earth. And the top of it reached heaven. And behold the angels of God were ascending and descending on it" (Gen. 28:12). The beauty was overwhelming. Peace was coursing through Ellen's bones because fear is not experienced there. She could tell the mission there was that His will would be done on earth as it was in heaven. In this dimension nothing else mattered. "Our Father who art in heaven, hallowed be your name, your kingdom come, your will be done, on earth as it is in heaven." (Matt. 6:9–10). "Forever, O Lord your word is forever settled in heaven" (Ps. 119:89).

Ellen was awestruck by the beauty radiating from the throne of grace, where Jesus was standing. She seemed to have lost the words to express it. He was not the picture she had in her mind, but humbly she said, "I have always loved you." Ellen looked at the lines in His face and the strength and surety in His eyes, and then she saw the scars on His hands. In her mind he had been a father to her. At the same time, she knew He was the Son of God because she knew He was the one who died for her. She was feeling the Holy Spirit's presence so strongly that she recognized Him on sight. Ellen looked up at Jesus and said, "Master, what could I possibly do for you?"

Jesus said, "Ellen, when I started making you, I was motivated by My love for you. I could not be prouder of you. You have been a faithful bride. What I called you up here for was to encourage you and to tell you that I will be calling on My faithful remnants to do exploits in My name. Some of you have been struggling with the enemy for years, not with where you were but with where God was taking you. Ellen, just as I awakened you, I will call the rest of the body to attention because we have some warfare to do. As time gets closer, the battle lines will be more defined. Do not be afraid because I can keep whatever is Mine. Faith and obedience is the key to bringing the armies of heaven to earth. I will not lose one of My children."

Ellen said, "I will do my best to obey."

When Ellen came back to the sense realm, she felt such peace that she was somewhat disappointed she had to return. She remembered animals talking freely. She thought even the rocks were praising God. "Jesus spoke of the disciples' praise, 'If these be quiet, the rocks and stones will cry out'" (Luke 19:40). She heard the blood of the martyrs crying out as well. "How long will it be before our blood is avenged?" (Rev. 6:10).

What a place to be, she thought, as she went back to bed. "Some of the scriptures I thought were just symbolic turned out to be exactly as He said they would be." Ellen felt as giddy as a bride.

Channing was Ellen's husband. It was so evident that God had put them together in marriage because the only thing stronger than their love for one another was their love for the Lord Jesus Christ. Channing and Ellen copastored a church in Bismarck, Arkansas, where worship and praise were always present, because God's glory resided there.

The Holy Spirit always shows up where love abides. God's glory shows up when God wants to fellowship with you and you respond with a longing to fellowship with Him, and that relationship pulls the glory down.

Ellen, Channing, and the Bismarck church have been preparing for this battle for years.

Channing was not surprised when Ellen told him of her encounter that day. He had been on the tractor all day cutting hay for the cattle and horses. Channing used this time on the tractor as sort of a prayer closet. The roar of the engine seemed to drown out the voice of his flesh so he could listen to the voice of the Holy Spirit. While Ellen was in heaven, Channing was on the tractor, meditating on the spirit world. *There has been so much activity lately in the invisible world,* Channing thought.

Ellen said to Channing, "It has never been about our ability as much as it has been about our obedience. The Lord has always met us there."

Channing agreed as he shut his eyes and went to sleep. He was not going to have a normal night's sleep.

As Channing slept that night, angels ministered to him about the spirit world. It was not just a place with angels and demons, as some see, but deeper than that—what he called the invisible realm. There is a realm where our thoughts are formed and pondered, a place in our minds where decisions are made such as *Yes, I will follow you, Lord,* or *No, I will not.* "For they that are after the flesh do mind the things of the flesh, but they that are after the spirit are after the things of the spirit. Repentance starts in our spirit and moves to our minds where the decision to turn or not to turn is made" (Rom. 8:5).

When he woke, he thought he had dreamed up a sermon. However, it was far more than a sermon. It was revelation knowledge that would lead him to places he had never been. God, through Channing and Ellen, was maintaining a group of believers made up of some of God's remnants who in short order would be used to change the course of the whole planet. There was such love flowing in their church that people were healed and delivered as they walked through the parking lot and in the door. It was the talk of heaven and earth. What a place to go. A hospital for heaven's soldiers is what they called it. Ellen and Channing were so humble that they seemed to be along for the ride the Holy Spirit was taking them on. They were not even conscious of the stir they had caused in heaven.

This is what humility is—when you lose yourself in your calling while doing the will of God, not even being aware of or caring what people are thinking because the Lord takes on your cares.

three

Let's Start at the Beginning

To give you some background about the spirit world, I, the one chosen to suffer until Christ is formed in you, will take you there and tell you some things that are rarely spoken of but far too easy to write about.

Heaven, even thousands of years ago, was a thriving, living, breathing place where you could feel the heartbeat of God. "Praise and worship were so natural, because in His presence is fullness of joy and at His right hand are pleasures forevermore" (Ps. 16:11). There were three archangels there: Michael, Gabriel, and Lucifer. There were innumerable other angels because Father God had so much going on.

Lucifer's job was to direct the heavenly choir, and somewhere in his anatomy was a harp. "Your pomp and magnificence are brought down to (the Underworld) along with the sound of your harps; the maggots (which prey on dead bodies) are spread out over you and worms cover you (O Babylonian Rulers). How have you fallen from heaven O light-bringer, day star and son of the morning! How have you been cut down to the ground, you who he weakened and laid low the nations, O blasphemous satanic king of Babylon?" (Isa. 14:11–12). He was the only angel with God's anointing. He stood tall and regal behind the throne of God, with his wings outstretched as antennae that seemed to draw strength from the praise and worship coming from around the many galaxies in the universes that God had created. All of heaven talked of the services and the majesty of the Father that were felt and seen in heaven's hallways.

Lucifer did not take the same look at the praise and worship that was coming forth the way the other angels did. Through his self-twisted mind, he began thinking that some of the praises belonged to him. After all, in Lucifer's mind he thought that he was the Father's best friend. Then Lucifer began stirring up trouble in heaven with lies and deceitful stories that questioned the holiness and authority of the Father. What he said was quite believable, yet lies and false words came out of his mouth. He deceived a third of the angels.

God the Father Himself had Lucifer and those angels cast out of heaven to a small planet that was without form, an empty waste, and darkness was upon the very deep places of the ocean. It was a place where Lucifer and all the fallen angels felt imprisoned. When they fell to earth, they made a bad planet even worse. They were seething with anger and rage, and they did not get along with one another. The drama and chaos seemed eternal. Lucifer lost all of his heavenly attributes and only ruled over fallen angels who hated him for deceiving them.

Lucifer's new name became Satan, because he was now an enemy of the Father. The fallen angels became demons, mindless creatures that would seek to vex, torment, and deceive the believer. Whether tormenting your mind or causing confusion and drama in your life, they had no bodies, so they would seek embodiment in animals and anything warm they could express themselves through.

"You were in Eden, the garden of God: chrysalises, beryl, onyx, sapphire, carbuncle, and emerald; and your settings and sockets were wrought in gold. On the day you were created you were prepared. You were the anointed cherub that covers with overshadowing wings, and I set you so. You were blameless in your ways from the day you were created until iniquity and guilt were found in you. Through the abundance of your commerce you were filled with lawlessness and violence and you sinned; therefore I cast you as a profane thing from the mountain of God and the guardian cherub drove you out from the midst of the stones of fire" (Ezek. 28:13–16).

Heaven was back to normal as soon as the cancers were removed. Satan forgot that it was impossible for God to fail at anything He did.

At an appointed time that no one knows but the Father, God began thinking about mankind. The Father, the Son of God, and the Holy Spirit had already created the heavens and the earth. The earth was a place without form, and void and darkness were on the deep places of the ocean. It was the place where Satan and all of the demons were imprisoned. God re-created the planet there. In the beginning (God began thinking about mankind) He formed, fashioned, and created the heavens and the earth. The earth (at that time) was without form and an empty waste, and darkness was on the face of the very deep.

"The spirit of God was moving and hovering over the face of the water" (Gen. 1:1–2). There was an incalculable amount of time between Genesis 1:1 and Genesis 1:2. He did re-create the earth in the six days following (Gen. 1:3–25).

God saw that their creation was good and came down from heaven to form man from the dust of the earth in the exact image of Himself, with his DNA. He breathed into the sand figure, and the image became a living, breathing human being, and God called him Adam. When Adam looked up at the Father, it was love at first sight. The intense love that the Father and Adam had for each other was unimaginable. They took Adam to the Garden of Eden, his new home. "Then the Lord God formed man from the dust of the ground and breathed into his nostrils the breath or spirit of life, and man became a living being" (Gen. 2:7).

Satan was enraged when he heard the news that Father God had made man with God's DNA. He was insane with jealousy and would, if he could, destroy what the Father had created: Adam.

God had made a race in His image and likeness. He had made a race of gods and given them dominion over the earth. "I said you are gods (since you judge as gods on my behalf, as my representatives); indeed, all of you are children of the most high. But you shall die as men and fall as men do" (Ps. 82:6–7).

four

Our Enemy

About the time I, the one chosen to suffer until Christ is formed in you, saw Satan's ferocity, a window opened before me, and I began to walk down a long hallway with rock walls. The air was thick and damp, and pictures of the forms and images that Satan had inspired were on the wall—Hollywood pictures portraying him as a Gothic monster with horns, claws, and thick skin in order to endure the heat of hell. However, that punishment would come later. Images of Nazi camps and weather perversions and scenes in history that he had caused were his entertainment.

The rumblings of the earth's plates were a constant reminder of the consummation of this age. Satan had taken on many forms in order to deceive. He is cunning and a master deceiver. I needed to be guarded and careful as I entered his presence. I pleaded the blood of Jesus as my shield and counted on our power of attorney, which was given to us when we first believed, to use Jesus's name with authority.

"Behold! I have given you authority and power to trample upon serpents and scorpions, and (physical and mental strength and ability) over all the power that the enemy (possesses) and nothing shall by any way harm you" (Luke 10:19).

I cannot tell you that I walked freely without fear. I had heard long ago that the word *fear* broken down means "a false emotion that appears real." I quickly checked myself, as I knew my only protection was through the blood of Jesus Christ and the faith and authority that I had in the way of Jesus's name that he bought for me through salvation. He loved me so much that I felt safe.

As I approached Satan, he was sitting at a large, table-sized desk. He was not as I had imagined. He looked like the most evil character imaginable. His demeanor reminded me of everything deceitful, assuming, hateful, rageful, and lust filled. I hated him on sight. He said he smelled fear on me.

I quickly said, "The Lord Jesus Christ, the one who sent me, saw you fall from heaven and will see you one day soon cast into the lake of fire." I questioned whether he was the worm that deceived the nations.

With an impudent look on his face, Satan said not to patronize him.

I was ready to leave, between the shifting of the earth's plates and the thunder-like sound they were causing me anxiety caused The pictures on the wall and the present company were beginning to make me feel exhausted. He was so sinister. I remembered in my own life how he would deceive me or use a weakness of my flesh to move right into my mind, to set up a kingdom or a vessel that he could use. I have to remember that it was my decision to do the deed and my weakness that caused it. After the deed, and the guilt and fruit of sin, what would we have ever done without Jesus? There would be no hope.

five

The Scourge of Sin

The Garden of Eden was a place where the Father and Adam could commune. They spent hours together. There was just as much peace and harmony in the Garden of Eden as there was in the city of heaven. The animals got along, and the plant life lived in harmony; everything was in balance. After a period of time, Adam wanted a partner. So God the Father put Adam to sleep and took bone and skin from Adam to make Eve. They were to be as one flesh and reproduce and repopulate the kingdom of God on earth as it was in heaven. They enjoyed one another's company as well as the company of the Father. It was heaven on earth, just as God had planned. God instructed Adam to name the animals and plants, and he did just as the Lord had commanded. "And God blessed them and said 'be fruitful, and multiply, and replenish the earth, and subdue it: and have dominion over the fish of the sea, and over the fowl of the air, and over every living thing that moves upon the earth'" (Gen. 1:28).

In the middle of the garden stood two tall trees, and everything the Father had made was beautiful. There were not too many rules that the Lord God had placed on Adam and Eve, except about these two trees. One of the trees was called the tree of life, and the other was called the tree of knowledge of good and evil. The Father said they could eat all the fruit they wanted from the tree of life. Father God had given them a strict commandment not to eat from the tree of knowledge of good and evil, for the day they ate from that tree, they would surely die.

Now the serpent was more subtle and crafty than any other beast the Lord God had made. He had four legs and was something to behold. He walked upright over to Eve and began talking to her. It was not so obvious that he was really the devil because all the animals in the garden talked. The serpent twisted the Father's words. He told Eve that God's motive in telling them not to eat the fruit of the tree of knowledge of good and evil was that God knew that the day they did, they would be as smart as the Father (knowing good from evil). Eve ate some fruit from the tree of knowledge of good and evil, and she gave some fruit to Adam, and he ate also. They committed treason against their Father God.

It is my personal belief that Adam and Eve, or Satan, never did hide anything from the Father. In fact, the Father had already sacrificed an innocent animal, tanned the hide, and threw it over Adam and Eve to cover their sin. If he had not done so, Satan would have killed Adam and Eve, and it would have been the end of the story. Satan would not only have gained God's planet but also his most precious creations, Adam and Eve. It was Adam and Eve's deed that turned the world over to Satan and put the scourge of sin on all the inhabitants of the planet. "For Adam and also his wife the Lord God made long coats (tunics) of skins and clothed them" (Gen. 3:21). Where did the Lord get them? He would have had to tan them in advance of the event. He had to shed innocent blood to cover their sin. That covering protected them from Satan killing them.

God turned to the serpent and pronounced two curses on him. "And the Lord God said to the serpent, 'Because you have done this. You are cursed above all (domestic) animals and above every (wild) living thing of the field; upon your belly you shall go, and you shall eat dust (and what it contains) all the days of your life'" (Gen. 3:14). The first curse was that he would lose his legs, which represented his authority and mobility, and have to crawl on his belly all the days of his life. The second curse was that his food source would be the dust of the earth. Mankind's flesh was made out of the dust of the earth. "Now those who are made of the dust are like him who was first made of the dust (earthly minded); and as is (the man) from heaven, so also (are those) who are of heaven (heavenly minded)" (1 Cor. 15:48, AMP).

As a believer I think that when we walk in the flesh (earthly minded) and not in the spirit (heavenly minded), we look like a food source for the demonic realm, and they come to torment, vex, and hinder us in the realm of our minds. He cannot possess us because of the indwelling Holy Spirit. That answers a lot of questions for me, such as why believers can have, at times, as much chaos and drama in their lives as unbelievers. Satan and his demons do not know what we are thinking, so they watch how we act and what we let come out of our mouths. When we do not control our carnal nature (the flesh), we become a food source for demons, and they start a feeding frenzy, creating havoc, drama, depression, oppression, vexation, guilt, and more. In my own life, I can remember a sin or deed I did forty or fifty years ago because, by my actions, I gave a demon the right to never let me forget.

When Satan lost his authority, he could not visibly appear. When he lost his mobility, he could not be everywhere at once; he had to depend on his demons to report to him. He only uses what we say and how we act to guess what we are thinking—he has no revelation knowledge. That curse came from him losing his mobility when he lost his legs in the garden.

If that were not bad enough, Adam, Eve, and Satan were cast from the Garden of Eden. God's war angels were put around the garden to keep them and the entire demonic realm from getting into or having access to the garden. The whole earth has never been the same since. The animals stopped talking because the event was so shocking.

Adam and Eve had to farm for their food. She would experience pain in childbirth. Sickness and disease would start its growth. Nothing worse could have happened. For the first time, Adam and Eve felt separation from the Father's love. Guilt and a constant feeling of unworthiness, like a dark veil, fell on them as a suffocating blanket. The separation anxiety must have been unbearable. Satan and all of his cohorts had a successful day because now the earth was his. All of creation has been paying for it ever since. Satan would love to make it the planet it was when he first fell. A planet void and without a form, with just darkness on the face of the deep, except now with lost mobility, and authority and a new food source (our sin nature—the flesh).

What Satan did not know was this: the whole planet runs on negative and positive energy forces. Even electricity runs from the negative to the positive. In our lives it has been the negative things that happen to us that herd us to the positive, where Jesus is standing there to help us get rid of the negative sin nature. Satan thinks he is so smart, but he never considered himself a pawn.

Have you ever wondered how many of us would have bitten Satan's hook? Mankind has never been loyal. Always remember that it does not matter how good someone looks on the outside; we all have sinned and come short of the glory of God. Some just hide it better. Do not put man on a pedestal because he will fall every time.

The Father's heart was broken as he pronounced to Satan, "You have deceived my children into knowing evil and dying spiritually so I will put separation between your seed and mine" (Gen. 3:15). "If I have to clear the slate and start all over, I will do it. If I have to come down myself, I will do it in order to take away your authority and power." Like a loving Father who looked down at His children and thought, *They're mine. You cannot have them without a fight.*

The Father knew that if anything was to be done, he would have to do it Himself, and he loved his creation so much, he had already made a plan. He had to do it legally and work through the minds and wills of fallen mankind. He loved his children and was prepared for battle in order to walk with his children as he did in the beginning with Adam and Eve.

The problem now was that mankind had died spiritually, and the Father had to deal with his children on a physical level and herd them, sometimes like cattle, through adversity. Through mankind's sin they had lost their connection. They had to be trained all over again.

Satan and his fallen angels were having a party. He knew something was up because the Father had never failed at anything. Satan wanted to destroy mankind because of his own jealousy. Satan hated losing the Father's attention when he fell from heaven, and he was worried now about some plan of salvation for mankind. That made him even more furious because Satan was never offered any forgiveness. His thoughts sent him into a flaming rage. God giving mankind His DNA and the possibility of salvation was maddening to Satan. He had no idea, because he did not see the future until he first read the Bible. Without any revelation knowledge, Satan's understanding was limited *six*

God Worked through Willful Mankind

The Father God went to work immediately through the minds and wills of men who would allow Him to use them. Mankind had lost the vision of what holiness even looked like. In fact, it looked like there was an evil lineage coming from the blood-line of Cain. The sons of God, or angels of God, came down to earth to give mankind a jump start in creating metallurgy and wheels and pulleys, farming, and basics that would have taken the people thousands of years to figure out.

God had given these sons of God, or angels, strict guidelines not to mate with the daughters of men, but they did anyway. That deed produced giants in the land. Then with Sodom and Gomorrah, evil became very prevalent, because Satan wanted to make God just give up and wipe out mankind completely. Things got so bad that God had to allow Noah's flood in order to break a genetic bloodline that Cain and the giants in the land had made.

Man had forgotten about God and had no standard for holiness, so He gave man the Ten Commandments through a prophet named Moses, showing God's basic laws, or His standard. Then God had man make a meeting place where a priest could go and offer sacrifices for sin. For without the sub-stitution, the death of something innocent and the shedding of its blood, there would be no remission of sin (just like in the garden with the tunics). God spoke through prophets and kings, and at times it seemed like there was no one defending or standing with Him. God used the sacrifice of animals until he could come down through the body of His son and take the sins away.

He would call His name Jesus because He would save His people from their sins. The Fatherhood of God felt it was not good enough to just take sin away. He could have done that in the beginning and just made mankind like angels. To be frank, He already had angels in heaven. He needed to understand sin's allurement. Who could tempt Him? Then who was holy enough to stand and judge Him? He wanted to come down to earth to be tempted and tried in all areas of life to show us how He could overcome. He wanted to be our kinsman redeemer, Emmanuel, which means "God with us." He never lost the desire to walk with us no matter the cost. We all could have used a fresh revelation of the depth of the Father's love that He has for His children, so John 3:16 had to begin, "For God so loved the world that He sent his only begotten Son [begotten, not made], Jesus, so that whosoever believes in Him would not perish but have eternal life."

seven

Jesus Finding Out
What It's Like to Be You

Think about the depth of Jesus's birth. He had to be born of a virgin who was impregnated by the Holy Spirit to retain God's DNA, because the child always has the Father's blood. Mary was born into sin. When Jesus was born, he was pushed from the womb of a woman, and God, in the person of His Son who had never slumbered, laid his head on Mary's chest and took a nap. He had never been sleepy, hungry, or tired. It was God finding out what it was like to be you and me.

As Jesus lived, He spent His life as a man but never sinned. He was the only being outside of God Himself that was able to keep God's laws. However, after he saw mankind and walked where we walked, he came up with a new kind of people who would be blessed.

In Deuteronomy 2814 God says, "If you will hearken to the voice of the Lord your God and do all that He commands you to do this day, you will be blessed." Read the verses Deuteronomy 28:15–68 tells of the curses that will befall us if we do not do all that He commands us to do. Wow, what a difference. Romans 8:1–2 says that there is now no condemnation for those who are in Christ Jesus if they walk not after the flesh and walk according to the spirit. The law of the spirit of life in Christ Jesus has made me free from the law of sin and death. Jesus freed us from the curse of the law because he became cursed for us. Every decree in the law was performance based as to who would be blessed or not. It seemed like if you had any problems at all, you would be cursed and never have a chance.

However, when Jesus sat where we sit, He came up with some new laws that had never been said before, found in Matthew 5:3–12. They were called the beatitudes, and they said, "Blessed are the poor for theirs is the kingdom of heaven, blessed are they that mourn for they shall be comforted, blessed are the long suffering for they shall inherit the earth, blessed are those that hunger and thirst after righteousness for they shall be filled, blessed are the merciful for they shall be shown mercy, blessed are the pure in heart for they shall see God, blessed are the peacemakers and maintainers of peace for they shall be called the sons of God, and blessed are those that are persecuted for righteousness' sake for theirs is the kingdom of heaven."

These statements lit the teachers and lawmakers up like a night-light because God had not said this until He sat where we sat and felt the pain we felt. I don't know about you, but that makes me love Him even more, because He loved me enough to find out what it was like to be me.

Later on we will learn that Jesus found out what it was like to be us so that we might love Him enough to want to learn what it would be like to be Him.

And usually there is suffering involved.

eight

Jesus Was Born to Die for Us

Jesus lived his life sinless, and John 21:25 (the last scripture in the book of John) says, "And there are also many other things that Jesus did. If they should be recorded one by one in detail, I suppose that even the world itself could not contain the books that would be written."

Nevertheless, the passions of Christ (death, burial, and resurrection) had to take place.

I wondered why they called Jesus's suffering before and during the cross His passion. His passion was taking the sins away; the cross was something he had to go through to do it. After Jesus rose from the dead and ascended to the Father, He shed His blood on the mercy seat in heaven, providing God's only acceptable sacrifice for sin whereby we might be saved.

Now we are saved by faith in what Jesus did for us. You just pray and ask the Lord Jesus Christ to come into your life and reveal Himself to you. You need to confess your sins and turn away, or repent. Then Jesus starts a cleansing process that may take a lifetime. You just have to be sincere, honest, and interested in Him and build a relationship with him that will last for eternity. It is just a miracle that He made it so easy.

nine

Who Is God?

God is a spirit. John 4:24 says God is a spirit (a spiritual being) and those who worship Him must worship Him in spirit and in truth (reality). "Jesus said to him, 'I am the way, the truth, and the life; no one comes to the Father except by and (through me. If you had known me (had learned to recognize me), you would have also known my Father. From now on, you have known Him and seen Him.' Philip said to Him, 'Lord, show us the Father (cause us to see the Father that is all we ask); then we shall be satisfied.' Jesus replied, 'Have I been with you so long a time, and you do not know and recognize me yet, Philip? Anyone who has seen me has seen the Father. How can you say then, "Show us the Father"?'" (John 14:6–9). Jesus is God in a bodily form, and the Holy Spirit is rarely seen in Jesus's earthly walk. We see them now as three personages and later as one God, and His name broken down looks like this: the Lord (the Father), Jesus (the Son), and Christ (the Anointed One or the Holy Spirit). At this point the disciples had not been introduced to the Holy Spirit.

The disciples were upset about Jesus leaving or ascending to the Father. "But because I have said these things to you (that I am leaving and going to the Father), sorrow has filled your hearts (taken complete possession of them). However, I am telling you nothing but the truth when I say it is profitable (good, expedient, advantageous) for you that I go away. Because If I do not go away the comforter (counselor, advocate, intercessor, strengthener, and standby) will not come to you (into close fellowship with you); but if I go away, I will send him to you (to be in close fellowship with you). And when He comes, He will convict and convince the world and bring demonstration to it about sin and about righteousness and about judgment. About sin because they do not believe in me (trust in, rely on, and adhere to me)" (John 16:6–9).

It was not until the day of Pentecost that they knew the Holy Ghost or the power of God, apart from Jesus and several visual events. From Pentecost forward came the name of the one God. When we get to heaven, we will see the Lord Jesus Christ. Now let's get back to what was happening.

ten

Springtime in AD 2014

It was Sunday in springtime, and on our way to church, the flowers smelled as if they were freshly cut. The smell was like perfume in the air. Greater than the fragrance of the flowers was the expectation of not just seeing my friends, but being in the presence of the Holy Spirit. There was an air of expectancy when we walked in. It felt like a rush that only the Holy Ghost could give. The church was packed, and praise and worship had begun. We immediately entered into worship and lost ourselves along with our worries and cares, laying them at the altar. Ellen was in the front row, and Channing was standing by his chair on the platform, worshiping as well. He never tried to compete with the presence of God. He flowed in the spirit and respected God's input. I have seen him go out of his way several times to obey the moving of the Holy Spirit. Today was no different.

The worship was a unified roar of praise when, as suddenly as it started, it stopped. When we minister to God in worship and it hits heaven, God responds with signs and wonders flowing through the gifts of the spirit. Mary, one of the members, wept in prayer as she gave a message in tongues—a language that is used between a believer and the Father that only the Father understands because it is spirit to spirit. When Mary quit, the crying stopped. There was a holy hush that fell across the crowd like a pulsing peace that let you know you were in the Father's presence. Frank Helms interpreted Mary's message:

"I will be doing a new transformation on the earth because I am going to wake up My bride. There will be a change in the level of holiness that the church operates in because in this transformation My bride is going to have to carry herself like a bride, by walking in holiness and wanting to be with her groom like a bride would. As always I will be transforming My people by the love I have for them. It will be the transforming power of that love that will transform the body of Christ." The crowd wept in praise because we could tell there were already some brides in the building.

I was happy about the word and sober about the responsibility of the new level we were going to in the spirit. I always heard, "Next level means a new devil." God always prepares us in advance for a major change.

Channing respectfully prayed and humbly said, "Let's open up God's Word in order to confirm the word we received from the Lord. Turn with me in your Bibles to Acts 1:8, where it reads, 'You shall receive power (ability, efficiency, and might) after the Holy Spirit has come upon you, and you shall be my witnesses in Jerusalem and all of Judea and Samaria and to the end (the very bounds) of the earth.'

"Acts 1:1–11 contain Jesus's parting instructions. Jesus was ascending to the Father. The disciples thought he was going to turn around and come back Himself because Jesus had already said in the book of John that the Holy Spirit, our comforter, could not come until He went to be with the Father. The disciples thought Jesus was the comforter. However, Jesus is telling us in Acts 1:8 that you shall receive power. The word 'power' comes from the Greek word *dunamis,* which is what the word 'dynamite'" comes from. Now some of us look like dynamite, and some of us look like smoke bombs. We all need to be looking like the bride of Christ and busying ourselves with being witnesses to the whole planet, or at least to our center of influence. The problem is that we do not look like the bride of

Christ anymore. I am not talking about all of us, but you know who you are. Look at the body of Christ today. We look like the world, smell like the world, and have the same chaos in our lives as the world. I have never really understood the reason why until I received a revelation while cutting hay this week.

"My spirit man went back to Genesis 3:14, when the Father pronounced the curses over the serpent. Adam and Eve had fallen, and the Father turned to the serpent and said to him, 'And because you did this thing, you are cursed over every living creature and every living thing upon the earth.' First he said the serpent (Satan) would lose his legs (authority and mobility) and crawl on his belly all of the days of his life (under the laws of the Father). The second command, I never understood until a few days ago. He said that his food source would be the dust of the earth. Now, what was mankind made out of but the dust of the earth? I think that even though we are believers, if we choose to walk in the flesh and not in the spirit, we look like a food source for demons to create havoc and chaos in our minds, and by doing so we are made to eat the fruit of sin.

"When Satan lost his legs, he lost mobility. He only knows what we say and how we act because he is not all knowing, all seeing, and he is not everywhere at once. That is why the church today could have the power of a stick of dynamite, but it looks like a smoke bomb. Look at Proverbs 6:2: 'You are snared by the words of your lips; you are caught by the speech of your mouth.' Or look at Matthew 12:37: 'For by your words will you be justified and acquitted and by your words you will be condemned and sentenced.'

"So holy living is very important because it keeps chaos, drama, and the works of the flesh from operating in our minds and working against our bodies. And most of all, it will keep demons from feeding on our minds. Besides, we need all of that to be serious about our appearance and look serious about our faith. I have never been much on preaching about clothes; however, men and women do not need to wear tight pants. We need to be dressing for the Lord Jesus. I bet if you ask Him what He would like to see you wear, you might feel a desire to at least be modest and ready for worship.

"The revelation that I received on the tractor the other night was about the invisible realm. Not just angels and demons. Have you ever believed that your thoughts or decisions are invisible when you say yes or no to the things of God or the workings of the devil? You choose how to act and make all your decisions there. It is the place of influence. Satan cannot possess a believer. But have you ever been vexed, confused, hindered, lead the wrong way, depressed, or made to feel a false sense of security when in reality you were looking like a fool to your peers? Could it be possible that you have been snared by the words of your mouth and by the actions that were not Christlike? You did that because in your (invisible) mind realm, you chose to follow demon influences instead of the Holy Spirit within you that came to convict the world of sin, righteousness, and judgment.

"Haven't we all? Maybe that's why we do not look like the bride anymore. Maybe that is why we have so much chaos, drama, mental illness, and physical problems."

Channing bowed his head and prayed: "I know, Lord, that You gave this to me because I needed to hear this as well. Thanks for revealing this to us so we can start looking and acting like Your bride. Now that we know the seat of Satan's influence and how he operates, we can guard our hearts and minds and watch what we say and how we act to make sure that we are doing our best to line up with the Word of God. Thanks for teaching us how to shut those evil voices down so we can listen only to the voice of the spirit."

Channing said he wanted everyone to come down to the altar to repent and ask the Father to remove any damage that we may have done to ourselves by our own decisions. Channing did not even get the invitation out of his mouth before the altars were flooded. The prayer service lasted for hours.

eleven

Up with the Force Field

When God asked Satan, "Have you considered my servant Job?" Satan had no phone book or GPS to look him up. Satan said, "I know the one; he fears God and hates evil." He must have stuck out like a sore thumb. Satan said he had tried to hit him, but God had put a hedge around him, a sort of force field that would not let Satan or his hellhounds in.

So it was with the Bismarck church. God had brought up the force field around the church, and there was talk of a twenty-four-hour prayer chain where there would be prayer twenty-four hours a day, seven days a week. Some brothers were heading it, and Satan was mad as hell about it. How was he going to find out what was going on if people minded their own business and got focused on spiritual warfare? That's the last thing he needed.

Sister Anna V. was an eighty-nine-year-old prayer warrior who came to church like clockwork. She was quiet and humble, and you never knew what she was thinking. Rule number one: never mistake humility for weakness. When she heard about the problems in the world, she instantly ran to "Bethel," an old chair that had been in her family for three generations. She prayed there when she had serious praying to do. Often she would pray in the spirit when she did not know how to pray. One day she was praying for the troops overseas. Even though she could not be there herself, she prayed just the same. I can see her in my mind's eye with her little hands on the wooden handle of the rocker. The finish on the handles had been rubbed through by her thumb and index figures. The texture of the wood, the smell of the chair, and memories of the past prayer warriors pushed her even harder to win. Heaven knew her name, and the angels often came just to watch her with amazement. Sister Anna V. had no idea.

Pastor Channing posted a giant clock in what we called the battlefield house but was actually a prayer room off the side of the church that he could leave open twenty-four hours a day. People in the church posted when they could commit to pray, and it wasn't too long before the clock was filled up. Now all we needed was a battle plan.

twelve

Repentance—the Power
of a Made-Up Mind

Pastor Channing was going away with Sister Ellen. They were going to a quiet place where they could get direction on where we needed to start.

Brother Albert spoke up and prayed for them, and he said that according to Hebrews 1:14, "Are not angels ministering spirits sent out to do service of God for the assistance of those who are to inherit salvation?" Albert knew that one could send a thousand of these angels to flight, and two could send ten thousand angels to flight. Albert said, "God, I don't know how many to send, but send enough to keep Ellen and Channing and give them wisdom and sound discernment. And then add enough to tell them where we should start." In Jesus's name he prayed.

Heaven was ablaze with activity as the angelic requests were being made. Angels were loading up to meet the request and demand that was made in faith by Albert. In addition, Anna V. prayed for a good four hours in the spirit, doing mighty exploits in Jesus's name.

Channing and Ellen headed out to a cabin on the other side of Mount Ida, Arkansas. Ellen fell asleep in Channing's lap as they rode down the winding road to the cabins. The first thing Channing prayed and felt in his spirit man was 2 Chronicles 7:14: "If my people that are called by my name would humble themselves and pray, crave and seek and require of necessity my face, and turn from their wicked ways, then will I hear from heaven and heal their land." The first problem to God seemed not to be the world but the church. Because God said if the church would clean up, he would take care of the world. Channing was led to God's list of six, no seven, things that God despises.

Proverbs 6:16–19 says, "These six things the Lord hates, indeed seven, are an abomination to him: a proud look (the spirit that makes one overestimate himself while underestimating others), a lying tongue, and hands that shed innocent blood. A heart that manufactures wicked thoughts and plans, feet that are swift to running to evil. A false witness who breathes out lies (even under oath) and he that sows discord among his brethren."

What stuck with Channing as he was meditating on these verses was that all of these sins are usually done with no one watching. In other words you could look clean like a saint when you are not.

I have said from the pulpit that in Pentecost I have seen plenty lost, and I can see why. Really, denomination has nothing to do with it. There are two groups: the saved and unsaved. Because most of us try hard to obey the Word of God and clean up our act, we concentrated for years on the outside of the cup, like the Pharisees, washing the outside of the cup while the inside was like dead men's bones. Most of the other churches did not do that, and because we looked holy, that made us overestimate ourselves or walk in pride. We even dressed plain and were persecuted as well. All of these seven things are done where decisions are made in the invisible realm. I have seen the meanest, most calculating people in churches, and the sweetest, most saintly, and usually not anything in between". Satan goes to bed early on Saturday night so he can get ready to go to church on Sunday.

1. A lying tongue. This has always been a bad thing. It is hard to remember what you have said or whom you said it to when you are a liar. Lying can ruin a life and make a person lose all his or her friends. It affects the one who lied and the one he or she lied about.

2. Hands that shed innocent blood. This could be the abortion of a baby, or what they want to call it today—the termination of a pregnancy. It could be mothers or fathers who shake a baby or smother it. On a larger scale, it could be a government that would put their young men in harm's way just to make a statement or to police the world. I sometimes wonder, just who do we think we are? If everyone keeps devaluing life, how hard would it be to put the elderly to sleep because they are using up too many Medicare dollars? It may sound farfetched, but if you read the regulations on some of the new health care bills, you would be shocked at the open doors. This is a big one—hands that shed innocent blood. God hates those who have blood on their hands, like those signing the bill that made it so.

3. A heart that manufactures wicked plans. I have seen this in the church or in business, when one person manipulates and controls all the people necessary to get his or her way. In church we have called it a jezebel spirit. In business I have seen people do wicked things to other people and say it is OK because it's just business. A man cannot serve God and mammon. If the Christian man does the right thing, God will step in and give him a bigger profit than he would make working evilly. Once again it started in a wicked person's mind, and his or her body executes it.

4. Many times in churches and in life I have found people who run to see an evil deed. I have in the back of my mind called them dirt devils. They like anything that stinks, such as the carnage of a broken church. I wonder if they would not be happier writing a column in the paper, calling it the "Hellhounds' Daily Record."

5. A false witness who breathes out lies under oath. Even with his or her hand on the Bible, is on God's hate list. The person had to be caught in the lie and dragged to court to be made to swear on the Bible, and he or she still told a lie. I believe if people would do that, then there is no telling what they would do to the people around them in their daily life or in a business deal.

6. All seven sins are bad. However, for someone to go into the church with the intent to sow discord among the brethren is shocking. How many churches have been wrecked, and how many people's reputations have been damaged? When I hear something, I try to squelch it as soon possible. We should all be on the same team, but sometimes you may think you're dealing with sheep until you see a few too many wolf bristles and find out they are wolves in sheep's clothing. I have seen many valid, thriving works of God happening, and then one that sows discord wherever he or she goes stops the revival with strange manipulations, like witchcraft.

All of these sins can be well hidden because they are lurking in someone's unguarded flesh, itching to come out through his or her mind or actions. We can hide all of this from men; however, nothing is hidden from God that will not be disclosed. Thanks be to God for His mercy and forgiveness toward us who believe.

thirteen

The Problem with the
World Is the Church

Channing received his revelation of the seven things that were an abomination to God. Channing and Ellen both marveled that these sins could linger in someone's mind for years and never get dealt with. People who should know better were abundant in these sins. Channing felt this would be a good place to start. Remember, we all have to work out our own salvation with fear and trembling. I always have checked myself for this first because we all surely need to stay off God's hate list of seven.

Channing and Ellen talked to each other, wondering how the Lord was going to pull all the churches together and draw anything out that looked like the bride. The church was so far removed from the appearance of a bride looking and waiting for her husband, the groom, to appear. What event in the Bible would bring them to that place? We had always been taught that it was the rapture of the church. Channing said, "It might be this very revival that we are in right now." They listened to the roar of Channing's old truck while they pondered what it might be.

Channing went out on the deck behind the cabin and sat down in one of two chairs while Ellen worked on getting us ready to leave. It was so quiet and peaceful that he could feel his heart beat and his own rhythmic breathing. The morning dew was on his hand, cooling it ever so lightly. The birds were singing, and wildlife was all around without the fear of harm. What a wonderful place God had made for us. What a beautiful planet. Ellen came out shortly and sat beside him. They both rocked back and forth in the chairs, just soaking up the presence of God. Life in their minds was wonderfully peaceful, and they both felt revived.

It was time to go back to Bismarck and get ready for the church service on Sunday morning. Channing wondered how the prayer warriors were doing and what had happened in the spirit while they were gone. Ellen wondered about the sisters in the church who had confided in her with their problems. In the back of Ellen's mind, she prayed for them often. Ellen and Channing were made for this job, and they loved every minute of it.

fourteen

Satan Has Not Been Idle

There was unrest in the spirit world. Satan had already sent some of his hellhounds to the Bismarck church; however, they could not get past the hedge of protection the Holy Ghost had put around it. Satan knew the Father had protected it for a reason, and he was looking for an opening in the believers' words to get in. Even the gossips in the church couldn't think of a thing to say. Satan was more watchful than normal, so he went down to Bismarck. There were some old angels he had known from before the fall working security, but do not fool yourself—they had not aged a bit. You see, Satan is not even popular in his own realm. What he did to the Father when he was cast out from heaven was enough. God's angels are fiercely loyal to God's people, and Satan did not want to be seen at all.

Satan went to do his other bidding, such as using people to manipulate weather patterns. He had used his weapons, like the Ionospheric Research Instrument, to unbalance the ionosphere. The weapon is in Alaska. The weather in California was as dry as anyone I know had ever seen it. It was as if the whole state was on fire. Just across the ocean, Satan had the Fukushima nuclear reactor that kept leaking radioactive hot water into the ocean. There had recently been radioactive hot water as close as Puget Sound. If that water ever made it to the sands of California, the nation's fruits and vegetables would be affected. Satan loved killing mankind and causing havoc wherever he went. His favorite tool wais apathy and deceit.

America was an easy target. He had always hated the Bill of Rights. He really liked a totalitarian government in which one person ruled—such as someone full of his demons. It made his job easier.

I sometimes worry about man trying to manipulate and play with delicate ecosystems that God set up. There has been a sharp rise in earthquakes. Seismic activity has been off the charts. Sin has taken a toll on the planet. I ran across an old scripture today that I could never understand or wrap my mind around until now. "The earth is utterly broken, the earth is rent asunder, the earth is shaken violently. The earth shall stagger like a drunken man and shall sway to and fro like a hammock: it's transgression shall lie heavily upon it and it shall fall and not rise again" (Isa. 24:19–20, AMP). I believe that the remnant of Christ will be with her Lord Jesus by then.

The American government has gotten out of hand with its spending. It is spending more money than it has. It almost seems like a conspiracy to take us down financially, except you cannot even get Congress to agree on anything. Our government is too big for a conspiracy.

There is a group of elitists that has grown over the years and has periodic summit meetings. It started out being called G-3 because it consisted of the wealthiest families in three countries. This group, now called G-20, controls the wealth of the world. Its members decide who rises and falls and who gets fed and who does not. Our Federal Reserve Board and five families that control the wealth of the United States come from this group. They are the groups that are behind what is spoken of as the new world order. We call it a one-world government. They are also pushing for a one-world religion. I cannot imagine what that would look like. Satan and his cohorts never miss a meeting. The pride and delusion that these people walk in are right up his alley. He has turned most of those projects to a sect of the demonic realm called principalities, powers, and spiritual wickedness in high places. This group will take the world down financially, making way for the Antichrist to fix it. I can see a plan coming together. If it were not for the restraining power of the Holy Ghost (in the church), we all would have no hope.

fifteen
When Is Jesus Coming Back?

"But of the exact day and hour no one knows, not even the angels of heaven, nor the Son, but only the Father. As it were in the days of Noah so will be the coming of the Son of man. For just as in those days before the flood they were eating and drinking. Men and women were given in marriage until the very day that Noah went into the ark. And then they did not know or understand until the flood came and swept them all away so will be the coming of the Son of man. At that time two men will be in the field and one will be taken and the other one left. Two women will be grinding at the hand mill: one will be taken and the other left. Watch therefore and give strict attention, be cautious and active for you do not know in what kind of a day, whether a near or remote one that your Lord is coming". (Matt. 24:36–44).

But understand this: had the householder known in what part of the night or morning the thief was coming, he would have watched and would not have allowed his house to be undermined and broken into. Therefore, you also must be ready; the Son of man is coming in an hour when you do not expect Him.

I never have had any clue to the day or the hour because even Jesus did not know. I did hear a rabbi say that in a Jewish wedding, the father of the groom would look down from his perspective to see if the bride was ready and then look at the son to make sure he had a place prepared for his bride. When everything was right, the father would tell the son to go get the bride. I believe the Lord has been waiting on the bride of Christ to be ready, looking like a bride and wanting to be with her husband.

I am in the same boat that you are. The Lord is calling His bride in an hour when we think not. We need to be ready.

sixteen

Stay Off God's Hate List, for Starters

As you walked into the Bismarck church, there was a glow of expectation on everyone's face, an air of expectancy, if you will, and waves of peace. Your eyes could have been closed, and you would have known where you were and whose presence you were in. The praise and worship had just started as people got to their feet and began to feast on His presence. Whatever you were going through and whatever had happened that week just left your mind and went to heaven in total surrender. For the next few minutes, it was all about Jesus. After all, He is the talk of heaven.

Channing walked up to the platform, so humbled by His presence. He wept and threw his hands up and wept some more. He knew God was taking them to a territory where they had not been and that was only traveled by prophets, and he certainly did not feel like he fit in their shoes. He felt like a regular guy.

Albert was a deacon for the church, and Channing and Ellen depended on him more than they could say. He was watchful for what the Holy Spirit was doing while he worshiped. Albert did not enjoy the spotlight. He believed his and his wife's ministry was to support the pastor and his wife. Albert's wife, Kim, ministered to women. She was a leader for women, and women naturally followed her. Albert was a leader as well. Men would listen to Albert when no one else could reach them. It was God's anointing on them both.

As the praise and worship closed, they took up the offerings and made the announcements. Channing got up to preach. He thanked the church for his and Ellen's vacation and began to talk about the things God said to him—that the problem with the world today is a sick church. He thought about what makes a sick church, and it was those six things—indeed, seven— the Lord hates and are an abomination to Him. He broke each one down to explain how they would manifest in a believer's life or in the world. He said, "Could it be possible that we are too proud to win the lost because we forgot where we came from?"

He ended the sermon by asking questions such as, "When was the last time you looked at someone and said, 'I am glad I am not where they are,' or 'I wonder why they act like they do'? So proud and arrogant we can look when we think we have arrived. Suddenly, when we have arrived, it seems like we quit caring about lost souls." He said, "I know there is no one here like that. I'm hearing a very weak amen.

"When was the last time you told a story, and at someone else's expense, you embellished the story until it became a lie? Have you told a lie about someone lately?

"Have you ever known someone was getting an abortion and stood by without saying a word? Have you ever murdered or thought about it? Hands that shed innocent blood are never talked about, but believe me when I say it is just well hidden.

"Have you ever had wicked thoughts? I mean you were driving down the road, thinking something of ill will toward someone in your past or present? Like a heart that manufactures wicked thoughts and plans? Maybe you are into pornography and are having wicked thoughts and making wicked plans. Have you ever set out to make a lustful thought into a real encounter?

"Have you ever heard of something awful, sinful, or stinky happening to a brother or sister, and you picked up the phone or ran like a bat out of hell to find out the latest? You really didn't care about the brother or sister. You may not walk a mile a day; however, your feet are swift to run to evil, and God hates it.

"Many people lie under oath, and I am sure it happens every day because people breathe out lies so easily when they are not under oath. In their minds, what's the difference? Well, I will tell you the difference. God hates someone who lies under oath, and it's obvious he or she does not respect the law.

"Have you ever met someone who triangulates every relationship in his or her life? He or she makes up lies to get two other people angry at each other and then walks away because the mission is accomplished. The purpose was to sow discord among the brethren. I have seen people willingly do it, and I have seen demons grab people's tongues, and before they knew it, those people were sowing discord among the brethren. If the shoe fits, take it off, because it is on God's hate list, and it borders on witchcraft.

"In fact, because so many of these sins are in God's people today, I am not even going to ask you if you have done any of these things because I know you have. Come on down here, and we will repent together."

People wept and cried with repentance as the Holy Ghost moved on them. They cried out to God and in some cases cried out to each other for forgiveness as needed. They were surely turning from their wicked ways.

That anointing did not stop there. As the day progressed into the night, service people felt chains breaking off their minds and curses being broken.

seventeen

Look Out, Satan! They're Up Again

No two women were moved more by the services than Sister Pat and Sister Sheila. Their prayers had always moved heaven, earth, and things under the earth. Pat came over to Sheila's house to sit by her pool in the mornings. The water was still and blue, the air was thick with dew, and they could hear all kinds of birds chirping. The garden Sheila had planted was stunning, and they both liked flowers. They sat down to meditate on the Lord and pray. They hardly got a word out of their mouths when the Holy Ghost showed up and began using their prayers like a weapon of words that would release the forces of heaven because they began to quote nothing but the Word of God. As they were talking, things were getting settled on earth as they were in heaven. They did not know it, but they were balancing the force of God's will being done on earth. We don't have any idea sometimes what a difference prayer can make. They were consumed with what they had to say because their minds were like the pen of a ready writer.

Both Sheila and Pat drew attention to the spirit world because when we speak the Word of God, the words continue going into the universe, doing exactly what the Father created them to do. In fact, a demon on Highway 70 screamed and said, "Look out—they are up again." It was afraid to get any closer to the house because Sheila and Pat didn't play when it came to prayer. They meant business.

Sheila prayed in an Iranian tongue and didn't know it. She had an impression at the time that she was stopping some terrorist act. Pat prayed with a sure resolution against some dark principality in high places. It is probably better that we do not know what we are praying when we are praying in the Holy Ghost because we are not praying to man but to God, releasing thousands of angels to do the warfare necessary to meet the aggressive demonic countermeasures. It would probably just make us proud.

The progress that the Bismarck church made ushered the presence of God into the earth so that mighty exploits could be done. I do not completely understand it. However, the Bible is the sum total of what God has said to those of us who believe. When we pray the Word, or what God has said, we are going to get results because God is not a man in that he should lie. In fact, he has never lied. The twenty-four-hour prayer team had not missed a beat.

Karlie and Richie started a mission in Hot Springs, Arkansas, called the Master's Touch. God put them together for a reason: to reach the unreachable and unteachable. Sounds like it would be impossible, doesn't it? For God nothing is impossible; it just takes a little while. They attend the Bismarck church; however, their own services are on Thursday nights, and don't kid yourself, the glory of God follows them. They let people with any problem come to the service as long as they do not try to use drugs or flaunt their addiction in the faces of other people who are trying to get to the place of repentance. Repentance is a work of the Holy Spirit because no one can come to the Father, save the Holy Spirit draws him or her. Their absence of pride is humbling. There is not an assuming one in the bunch. The hope is that the Holy Ghost, who came to convict the world of sin, righteousness, and judgment, will be enough to change the people's minds to turn the other way. It is easier to catch a fish than clean one. We have never been able to clean anyone anyway. It has to be done from the inside out. If you try to make someone change, they will only resent it, and usually it makes things worse.

Spirits of sorcery had to move out of the location of the Master's Touch because Karlie, Richie, and the Bismarck church were sending them fleeing for their lives. The people came in the door with their sin and habits. Some of them knew the Lord and some didn't. However, it was a package deal—with their sin came the particular drama and chaos that the people didn't really realize they were walking in until they got a taste of freedom. You have to be a very long-suffering individual to hang out with addicted people until Christ is forms in them. To get through it, sometimes you have to treat it like a job and hold on to them and love them until they are delivered. The job is flesh killing. Richie and Karlie loved it. When the Father has something really hard to do, who does He have to call on but His believers? The rest are doing their thing or just dealing with their own problems because everybody has been tempted to do something they didn't want to do. Some people are just very good at hiding their demons.

eighteen

It's Getting Hot in Here, so Keep On All Your Clothes

There are five prisons that make up the complex of hell: the lake of fire, hell, the bottomless pit, Abraham's Bosom, and the abode of the dead. Hell has always been a place of torment. The Bible talks a lot about hell, such as who will be there and the degree of punishment he or she will receive according to his or her deed. Satan and some of his untrusting cohorts were planning a meeting there. Even when they get together they do not get along.

They met at the door to the bottomless pit. The air outside was thick and full of the smoke from the pit. The only beings bound there were the Nephilim, the sons of God who mated with the daughters of men, which produced giants in the land. This was before Noah's flood. They all hated that the Nephilim talked all the time and did not keep their word. This was the pot calling the kettle black.

When Satan took the floor, the demons and fallen angels sat down to listen. Even though they did not trust him, he was still their ruler. Satan spoke of revivals that had started all over the world. He mentioned the Bismarck church with his usual disdain. He wanted to make sure his demons named Pride and Dissension were aware of the situation, along with other spirits he knew could split a church. He said their time was short, and if they were going to win this battle, they would have to make men and nations argue enough to go to war. The hope was that mankind would destroy itself.

Satan worked on weather modification and broadcasting chemicals that would quicken the dying process of the human race. Satan could tell time was short because the planet was showing signs of age with earthquakes, sinkholes, plate movements, and violent storms. Satan, even without revelation knowledge, was afraid he was running out of time as he read the Bible. He still acted as if he was smarter than the Father; however, Satan knows that's a lie because Satan has no revelation knowledge.

The G-20 summit started this week, and Satan never missed it. The wealthiest people in the world were there, as well as their representatives. Satan took with him several proud demons called the "deceitfulness of riches," so everyone would feel superior to the common man, ensuring the common man's ability to gain wealth would be weakened. Satan is in his element when people are either prideful or suffering. He thrives on making people have the wrong opinion of themselves. If he can't get someone to be prideful or delusional, he is OK with people suffering. All there will be in hell is suffering, torment, and drama without remedy.

Remember, in the afterlife there will only be those who are saved from hell through faith in Jesus Christ's finished work on Calvary. The people who refused to accept Jesus Christ as the sacrifice God accepted will go to hell. God does not send people to hell—they send themselves. One of Satan's biggest tricks is to make God look like a wicked judge, but the Father is the only one worthy to judge. There will be only saints and nonsaints because the Father has given mankind thousands of chances.

Satan left the G-20 summit laughing as he said, "The deceitfulness of riches gets them every time." His favorite vices are lust of the flesh, lust of the eyes, and pride of life. Satan laughed as he said, "It's been working for years."

Satan and his demons had a feeding frenzy, just like piranhas, as they fed on the works of the flesh in full force at the

G-20 summit. You could see the demons leaving with the dust of the flesh dripping from their mouths like mud. They showed no restraint.

Satan said, "It is not usually this easy."

Gluttony cried, "Why do we have to leave so soon?"

nineteen

Israel Will Be the Stage

There is no property on the planet dearer to the heart of God than Israel. The covenant that God made with Abraham thousands of years ago is still alive today. Israel has God's attention twenty-four hours a day, and His watchful hand is still on the Jewish race as God's chosen people. The Jews needed a place they could come home to, and in 1948, Israel became a nation. The Jews who had been scattered all over the earth had a place to go home to, and they were coming in droves.

Along with the good was the bad—Muslims and Christians living next door to each other. The Muslims and Christians have never gotten along. There has always been contention over the land and whom it belonged to. Complicating things more, Christian and Muslim holy sites are very close and intertwined. Satan and the Muslims have hated the Jews and in fact have declared a holy war against the Christians and Jews. They have not understood that we wrestle not against flesh and blood but against principalities and powers and spiritual wickedness in high places. They call the United States the great Satan because our support to Israel has been unshakable. America has become more wicked in the last thirty years than I ever thought possible.

Radical groups of Muslims appear to be planning to destroy Israel. I first heard about this after the attacks on 9/11 took place at the twin towers in New York. They have been at the core of multiple bombings around the world, and have increased in number enough to try to take over Iraq and then move to Iran. Several other countries financially support them to do this job.

For years Iran has been attempting to make weapons-grade plutonium for dirty bombs or even a nuclear warhead. I still say the Russian factories that make weapons-grade plutonium have never closed down, even through the Cold War. In fact, I do not think they have stopped making any weapons. They probably sell to any buyer. The communist agenda has never changed. Iran would destroy Israel if it could, but God the Father would never allow it.

It is supernatural to me that one country, Israel, has drawn more attention than any other country on the planet. Some of the present leadership in the United States believes that we should declare Israel an international country and all of her religious sites as international property. They want to put Israel under the control of the United Nations. That same group wants one world religion because they do not stand for anything. There is not too much that needs to happen to start the countdown to the second coming of Christ. The Muslims are looking for a return, and some of the Jews are still looking for a savior. They may have to settle for the Antichrist and seven years of tribulation such as the world has not known. Believe me, the world has seen a lot of tribulation.

The area of Iran and Iraq has been referred to as Satan's seat. The devil has kept these regions inflamed for six thousand years. Satan thinks he is so smart because he possibly correlated all of these events.

God wrote His book of how things would end from the beginning. Nothing ever has caught Him off guard.

twenty

Economic Collapse, and Who Is the Antichrist?

There is general restlessness globally. Countries' currencies are failing because their social programs went from being helping hands to becoming entitlements.

Ever since the North American Free Trade Agreement (NAFTA), there has been an awful trade imbalance with the rest of the world. It was done in order to redistribute wealth to poorer countries. Now we owe China billions of dollars, and if the United States does not pay them back, China could recall their note and attempt to take the United States over under international law. Printing enough money to pay China back would take our dollar bill to a worth of twenty-five cents. Inflation would be out of control.

America has been dependent on credit for years. The money owed to Japan and China is just to cover the interest on social security loans. The United States allowed the Chinese government to buy half the ports in California. Japan owns a lot of land and businesses in the United States. I believe that by making several decisions against the laws of God, judgment is coming to America. America would like us to go cashless because the government could give you the mark of the beast and you could not receive or spend money without using the number. No one could make a financial transaction without the government knowing about it. The selling point would be no bad checks and no missed or hidden income; therefore, more taxes and more government control.

Things are going to get so bad globally that the world will be looking for a savior. Instead they will get the Antichrist. His cohort will be a false prophet, and they will deceive the nations. The United Nations and their army of UN peacekeepers do not care what country they are in; they will just follow their orders.

Here is a list of names and attributes from the Dake Annotated Reference Bible that may help us to identify the Antichrist: "Anti-Christ" (1 John 2:18), "The Assyrian" (Isa. 10:20–27), "the King of Babylon" (Isa. 14:4), "the Spoiler" (Isa. 16:4),; "The Extortion" (Isa. 16:4), "Gog—the Chief Prince of Meshach and Tubal" (Ezek. 38:2–3),; "the Little Horn" (Dan. 7:8, 24 8:9, 23), "King of Fierce Countenance" (Dan. 8:23), "the Prince that shall come" (Dan. 9:26–27), "the King of the North" (Dan. 11:5–45), "The Man of Sin" (2 Thess. 2:1–12), "the wicked" (Isa. 11:4), and "The Beast" (Dan. 7:11 and Rev. 13).

"The Anti-Christ will be called the Man of Sin because he will be lawlessness embodied. The leader in a great falling away of the Christian faith. He will be called the son of perdition because he sold his soul to the devil" (Rev. 11:37–39).

In 2 Thessalonians 2:3–12, it reads, "He is to be revealed. He will be the opposer of God. He will exalt himself above God. Will accept worship as God. His worship will be carried on at the future temple site in Jerusalem. He will claim to be God. He has a time to be revealed. Something is now restraining him being revealed" (the Word of God, the restraining power of the Holy Ghost, the bride of Christ's presence on earth, or the governments aligning). Verse 7 uses a lowercase *h* in "he" so we know it is not the Lord. I personally believe that the Antichrist cannot be revealed until "the meaning of the church is taken away. He is a man, for he will be killed by Christ at the battle of Armageddon." He will be Satan's agent, used to set up the last world dictator. He will perform lying wonders or miracles by the power of Satan. He will be a deceiver. Only those who are lost will follow him. The reason that men will be deceived is that they will reject truth, love sin, and refuse salvation. He will be great at delusion and lies. He sounds like the devil's son to me.

twenty-one

From Bismarck to Hot Springs

Ellen, Channing, and the Bismarck church were invited to share what had been happening at Bismarck. Word had spread rapidly that Bismarck had fresh fire from the altar of God spill into the building. It seems like they had the right combination: hunger and thirst for more of the Lord, humility, and respect for the Holy Spirit's presence and the laws of God or at least the Ten Commandments. The love the people had for one another created an environment where someone could go to the altar at any time and never be judged. The presence was so strong that people would come on their breaks from work just to soak in His presence. It's really all about a love affair that we have with the Lord Jesus, like a bride would have for her groom.

Outside of the twenty-four-hour prayer service, people showed up at the church at all hours. They walked in the door and fell on the floor in worship, soaking up the presence of God. Although it may have looked strange to the flesh, it was refreshing to the body and spirit. Reports of people getting healed in the parking lot were very common. Sometimes there were strange manifestations of the spirit, such as moaning and travails and many sounds that only heaven understands. We don't understand them, but heaven does, and that's good enough for me. Who am I to judge what the Holy Ghost is doing?

Channing and Ellen just held tightly to each other because they knew that it had nothing to do with them. This was bigger than they were. It was simply about loving the Lord and Him loving them back.

The church was one of the largest congregations in Hot Springs, Arkansas. It was the evening service, and the Holy Spirit showed up and showed off right away. The worship was amazing, and all of the people who loved to be in the presence of God were worshiping. Then there were those who didn't want to or didn't feel like worshiping; they stood in apathy. In the back of the church, people used their phones and wrote on pads, drawing pictures.

Satan and all his usual hellhounds were there. They heard about it from the talk in town. His demon Apathy was already working the crowd. Jealousy and Competition had one deacon questioning the validity of it all. Some thought that this was something that would come and go. Some were ready to go when they got there. Hater and Backbiter were attacking the minds. Satan made sure he brought anything possible to quench the spirit. He even brought Dirt Devil to see if he could dig up something from anyone's past that went to the Bismarck church. Satan was glad Ellen and Channing were out of their normal environment and away from the hedge God placed around them, surrounded by people who loved them.

Channing got up and boldly gave testimony about the dreams, visions, and supernatural encounters that made the Bismarck church. He brought up the number of people who hungered and thirsted after righteousness. They had teachings about how to be and look like the bride of Christ, not only by professing their faith but also by turning from their wicked ways, making their hearts teachable and reachable to Jesus. He said he felt we needed to go back to the basics, and that we somehow had lost our anchor in Christ and were being swayed by the lust of the flesh, lust of the eyes, and the pride of life.

With that, Satan and his demons had some people rolling their eyes, sighing, and letting Channing know they had a tic. Channing had seen this happen before. He always believed that we could catch a fish, but the Lord Jesus had to clean it. Their actions let him know that they felt their roles in the church were to be critics.

Even while Satan was attacking the service, he knew he had lost when suddenly war angels and the Holy Ghost showed up. The worshipers could not help themselves; they just started doing what they do. The power of God knocked the place sideways with a demonstration of signs and wonders that could not be denied. Satan and his pets, as well as his implants in the church, had to leave because they could not take it anymore. After all, they thought that heaven was supposed to clap just because they showed up. They simply did not get it in the first place—that was the problem.

The Bismarck church had started something at the Hot Springs church that was not stoppable by man or demon. The book of Acts had started all over again, and the news was spreading like wildfire.

twenty-two

Last-Day Revival or
Great Falling Away

Channing and Ellen went by the church to pray at their appointed time on the prayer clock. This month it was from three until four in the morning, and they had left the children's church building open for prayer. They grabbed two lawn chairs to sit outside the church to pray.

The air was warm, and the trees were swaying in the wind as if there were storms coming. They felt a warm blast of air soon followed by a cool blast. The sky was still, clear as glass, with millions of stars.

Channing said, "This looks so big, and we are so small."

Ellen said, "God called us to this, and He equipped us for it."

Channing said to Ellen that he was just talking about the sky.

She said, "Let's get serious."

They sought the Lord, praying about the request from the congregation and then lost themselves in worship. Suddenly, they felt something downloaded from heaven directly to their spirit. Before they knew it, two hours had passed, and people pulled up in the parking lot to relieve them. Ellen and Channing were still numbed by the encounter. They spoke to the members and then left. Neither of them could even talk about it until later because it was surely a message delivered by the Holy Ghost and written by the Lord Jesus Christ. Channing looked at Ellen and wondered what was next.

Channing and Ellen went home to go back to bed for a while. However, they were both excited and apprehensive because the words that the Father said were so plain, they triggered the fear of God in their life.

The churches today have lost the fear of God. They love the grace of God and are grateful for it. But have we ever seen the judgment of God on sin? The closest thing I know to what judgment feels like was when the Lord disciplined me for something I had done wrong or moved me from some sort of sinful pattern to a place of repentance. He still hates sin, and don't forget it.

When Ellen and Channing received their download, they were shocked as they compared notes because they received the same message without losing anything in translation or inter-pretation. Even their personalities did not lead them to misin-terpret the word.

They had received the message that this fresh fire would spread like wildfire through all denominations, cultures, and backgrounds. The rich and poor would be offered the same anointing. I am not talking about the gifts of the Holy Spirit, as some will automatically think, although they will still be avail-able and used as ministry gifts. This fresh fire from the altar will be a baptism of fire that will separate the dross out of the gold. Right and wrong is on its way back. There will be a trans-forming power like the world has never seen as God wakes up His body of believers, His remnants that listen and obey.

I know this sounds wonderful, but the fresh fire will make people go back to the basics of our faith. There will be a lot of absolutes, and with that will come persecutions such as we have not seen in years. People are fine with Christians as long as they stay in their own church and do not make a stand or push their belief system on anyone. This fire will burn up apathy. This will go to Washington and around the world and make the wheat look like wheat and the chaff look like chaff. The light alone contained in it will make the darkness flee.

Jesus came to find out what it was like to be us. Now we are going to see what it was like to be Him. If you want to reign with him, you must suffer with Him. It will be a natural thing to do when the fire takes hold and burns the flesh and carnal nature from us. It will not be needless pain.

Channing said it is two-edged swords that will make a sinner stick out as a sinner and a saint stand up like a saint. It will cause the church to fall in love with Jesus all over again and look like the bride and body of Christ.

The more Ellen and Channing thought about it, the more sobering it was. This was not just a revival—it was a *last-day's revival*. However, this could be a revival and a great falling away at the same time, as only time would tell.

twenty-three

Something's Up in Heaven

Satan had some fallen angels trying to figure out what was going on in heaven. There were angels flying out in formation to position themselves around the churches and spiritual centers in the world, so when this fire hit, they would be there before Satan's minions could react. Satan and all of hell had no idea that we were this close to his destruction. They were completely confused and caught off guard, as they thought they had all of these Christians under control, full of apathy, and not standing for anything—easy prey that did not fight back. As they came back to where Satan was to report their findings, they argued over who would tell him because they knew he would be enraged—and enraged was not a strong enough word. He started screaming blaspheming words and remarks that only a calculating devil could say. The venom of his dilemma was running down the side of his face, back to his fall from heaven; the creation of man with God's DNA; and, last but not least, his remarks about the birth, death, and resurrection of what he called the bastard son of Mary. He still did not believe in the virgin birth because he was convinced he would have never missed that happening. In fact, with that, Satan decided to start with pastors in the churches that snicker at the idea of a virgin birth. He left in a fury with trails of smoke and venom sliding out of his mouth, in hope that he could increase the delusion in the churches that he still held captive.

All the demons were hiding out as Satan had one of his tantrums like a baby. He hates his own and always has. He tempts and deceives out of hatred for God. His favorite thing to do is hurt the creation of God and make it look like God allowed it or did it himself. He has caused suffering and blamed God for it. After all, long ago they were deceived by him as well. Do not feel sorry for them, because they would do it again if given the chance.

twenty-four

A Brewing Battle Is Coming

All of heaven was at attention and alive with activity as the war angels were getting ready by sharpening their swords. With their faith in the Lord Jesus Christ, they were ready to fight with the sword of the spirit, which is the Word of God. It cannot fail. Creatures of all types, sizes, and shapes around the throne were not idle. They were worshiping the Father for the victory in advance, as if they already knew the outcome.

The principalities and powers, as well as spiritual wickedness in high places, were at Satan's command. The angels of God outnumbered the demonic realm of influence three to one. Some of the problems that God's army was facing were not just in the demonic realm but also in the believer and nonbeliever. The power of a made-up mind to either follow God's will or not is a strong force as well.

For centuries the Holy Spirit has visited churches of all denominations, and God showed up with a word for that time, and instead of continuing to follow the Lord onto the next revelation, they stopped and made a denomination out of that series of revelations. The Holy Spirit wanted to take the church further and was stopped by disbelief. I have seen the Holy Spirit blocked at the door. The Holy Spirit will never stay where He is not welcomed, and I have rarely seen Him show up again at the same place. This time it was going to be a mandate from heaven for one last appearance with such power that it would make what was hidden come out into the open. It would make the true believers more evident and the false believers go home because they believed with their minds, but their hearts were far from it. God was drawing the line in the sand by breaking the yoke of bondage and seeing if they would still follow. This would be like letting the dove out of the cage, and the Holy Spirit would have no restraint. I believed that people would either love or hate it.

Remember that the last group that was in heaven had never been tested. These were the angels and all of the created beings that were in heaven until iniquity was found in them. I believe that God is not going to ever allow a fall again. Every saint will be tested so that the saint will know what is inside him- or herself. God already knows, but the fire will reveal it. It will make the evil name itself. The fire makes the believer ask, "Who am I, and what is my name?" The fire of the Holy Spirit will reveal your weakness so you can deal with it.

twenty-five

The Awesome Awakening
of the Church

It seemed like a normal Sunday at the Bismarck church. All of the faithful members were there as well as some of the visitors that usually only come on Christmas or Easter, so the house was full. Channing and Ellen were still expecting the Holy Spirit to show up as they were briefed by the download the other night. There was an air of expectancy as always at the Bismarck church. The service started as Channing taught Sunday school in the main sanctuary and moved right into the service at ten thirty. The spirit and the anointing were strong as the worship began. It moved according to course until everyone suddenly got very quiet. Channing and Ellen were expecting a message and interpretation from the Lord as usual to confirm the word. Nothing seemed to happen, so the church just waited in silence.

Without a warning angels became visible, lining the walls of the church as the Holy Spirit showed up and began to walk up and down the aisles, as well as up on the platform. Ellen and Channing were both quickened in the spirit along with all the worship leaders. People were letting go of demons while others were hitting the door because of fear. The conviction was overwhelming. People were instantly healed, and even the elders and older disabled members were throwing down their walking sticks and walkers because the Holy Spirit said it was time not to retire but to rededicate their lives as the Holy Ghost renewed their physical bodies a good twenty years, renewing their faith and calling for these last days. There was more genuine repentance and revival than I had ever seen. We all thought it was just for the Bismarck church. Manifestations like I had never seen, moaning, howling, and groaning in the spirit that you would not dare question as the Holy Spirit without restraint was allowed to move. The Holy Spirit became God's unrestrained love. The anointing would flow through us in repeated pulses that left us changed.

Fire was seen as a heat signature coming out of heaven to hundreds of thousands of places on the planet. The military was talking about it, and all nations were on alert as if we were under attack by some alien force. But when the Holy Spirit hit locations with people who were seeing the heat signature, reports similar to those from Bismarck were taking place while they were on the job. People were crying out to God without provocation. Some thought it was the end of the world.

A missionary ministering to one tribe in Africa who had been cutting their arms to get their god's attention had a revelation that Jesus Christ had already been cut for them; they looked down, and the cuts were gone as well as the scars. It was on national television around the world. We could not turn the channel without regular entertainment being interrupted by special reports.

These were just some of the good things that were happening. People were in the street thinking the world was going to end and that this was a prerequisite to an alien attack. What was alien, foreign, and unfamiliar to them was anything but to us.

More people's lives were changed in this one visitation than ever before. Powerful people were struck in the United States, and people who had been watered down were not watered down any longer. The fire of God had certainly hit the altars of every meeting place, and some were dragging their altars from the basement and putting them out again. The church of the Lord Jesus Christ was more alive now than ever.

Who would have ever thought that all of this could start with remnants of believers who were just so in love with Jesus that He had consumed all their thoughts and actions? He loved us all into submission. I am not only talking about the Bismarck church, for God has always had remnants in nearly every place. After all, it was the remnants who knew their authority in Jesus's name who had been restraining evil through prayer for thousands of years. The Holy Spirit and His angels knew them well. Some of the believers had no idea they were part of the remnants because they were too busy seeking the Lord on the behalf of others, sometimes even forgetting about their own needs. That's what remnants do.

twenty-six

Great Revelations and
Some Failed Expectations

The television screens around the world were lit up with news reports. Some instilled fear that it was some sort of alien encounter. The heat signatures were too calculated to be a natural disaster, the news media declared. People talked about alien implants. The stories spread like wildfire.

The Cable News Network (CNN) mocked the right-wing conservatives, saying we thought it was a move from God. The commentator stated that Al Gore said it was a side effect of global warming. They had no idea how hot it was going to get before this was over.

More important than the news media was the effect it had on the Christian community. Most Christians were moved to a genuine place of repentance and a type of commitment that the apostles had when they saw Jesus die and resurrect from the dead. They were prepared by the spirit instantly for whatever persecution would come, and believe me, we could feel it coming.

The Muslims talked about a prophet coming, and the Jews thought their messiah was going to show himself.

Every religion on the planet tied this one event to their hope for a coming entity.

Do not forget 2 Thessalonians 3:7–10: "For the mystery of lawlessness (that hidden principle of rebellion against constituted authority) is already at work in the world, (but it is) restrained only until he (the church) who restrains is taken out of the way. And then the lawless one (the Antichrist) will be revealed and the Lord Jesus will slay him with the breath of His mouth and bring him to an end by His appearing at His coming. The coming (of the Antichrist) is through the activity and working of Satan and will be attended by great power and all sorts of (pretended) miracles and signs and delusive marvels— (all of them) lying wonders. And by unlimited seduction to evil and with all wicked deception for those who are perishing (going to perdition) because they did not welcome the truth but refused to love it that they might be saved."

This was a time of great revelation from God and a time of great deception from Satan.

twenty-seven

What Are We to Fight With?

Long ago God gave the church nine gifts of the spirit for ministry and warfare against our adversary, the devil. Since the recent outpouring of fresh fire from the altar of God, these gifts of the spirit have been increased in power to match the coming battle.

You will find these gifts mentioned in 1 Corinthians 12:7–11:AMP "But to each one (believer) there is given the manifestation of the Holy Spirit (the evidence and illumination of the spirit) for the good and profit for all. To one is given in and through the (Holy) Spirit (the power to) speak a message of wisdom (we call this gift the word of wisdom). To another (the power to express) a word of knowledge and understanding according to the same Holy Spirit (we call this the word of wisdom). To another (wonder working) faith by the same (Holy) Spirit (we call this the gift of wonderworking faith). To another the extraordinary power of healing by the one Holy Spirit (we call this the gift of healing). To another the working of miracles (we call this the gift of miracles). To another prophetic insight (the gift of interpreting the divine will and purpose; we call this the gift of prophecy). To another the ability to discern between (the utterance of true) spirits and (false) spirits (we call this gift discerning of spirits). To another various kind of unknown tongues (we call this the gift of tongues). To another the ability to interpret such tongues (we call this interpretation of tongues). All these (gifts, abilities, and achievements) are brought to pass by one and the same (Holy) Spirit, who apportions to each person individually as He chooses."

For nearly every weapon of warfare that God has, the devil has a counterfeit. This is a list of the gifts of the spirit.

- For God's gift the word of wisdom—Satan has the ability to tell something he has heard, which is usually a lie or deception.
- For God's gift the word of knowledge—Satan's gift would be fortune-telling, which is usually received by some form of carnality that he or one of his cohorts has seen.
- For God's gift of wonderworking faith—Satan would use fear to produce a lying wonder.
- For God's gift of healing—Satan's counter is sorcery.
- For God's gift of miracles—Satan produces more lying wonders or deceptions.
- For God's gift of prophecy—Satan would manipulate and lie by the use of witchcraft.
- Satan has no match for the unknown tongue because he cannot understand. It is a language between the believer's spirit and God. There is no way Satan could interpret it.

Every believer in Jesus Christ has these abilities available for the asking. God does not have a bad or unnecessary gift that has no real purpose. They were given to the church for ministry and warfare. I could see if you were a believer who never wanted to minister or enter warfare and had no intention of doing anything in return for all that Jesus has done for you not seeing these gifts as necessary. If you are one of those people, do not worry—you will not operate in one of the gifts of the Holy Spirit. They are not for you. These gifts are for ministry or warfare. I always needed every tool I could get. When you have to work in hell's kitchen, you need to know where all the pots and pans are. There has never been a time in history that the gifts of the Holy Spirit were used in the manner that they will soon be used. The most powerful weapon we have is the Word of God, and we must live our lives in such a way that we respect holy living. Whatever God tells you to do or whatever has been revealed to you, walk in it. You will then be unstoppable.

twenty-eight

Satan Is Getting Ready for the Battle

Satan had a command post underground next to the Dome of the Rock in Israel. He wanted to be near the place where the Antichrist would soon appear. Down the street a new temple was erected for animal sacrifices. Only the Jews that did not believe God's son himself, in the person of Jesus Christ, was the final atonement for sin still felt the need for this blood sacrifice. Satan loved the fact that he had blinded their eyes to the point they could not believe the Gospel and be saved. In addition, Satan knew a lot would be happening in Israel in the last days.

From Satan's command post, he sent out hellhounds and demons to areas that were alive with the Holy Spirit as well as to places of great delusion so that some would believe a lie and be damned. Around the clock they worked to discredit God's move and undercut His motives. The fear they felt by the most recent events was their motivation to stop time if they could. At this point they could smell hell, which would be their eternal place of punishment. Their time was running out, and they knew it.

The transformation that had followed the fresh fire in America had affected everything. Congressmen and senators were doing everything they could to get America on the right track again, but with their renewed minds working, not everyone was happy about it. They overturned Roe v. Wade (the abortion bill). They changed gay marriages to civil unions.

They prayed about every decision instead of listening to the pocketbooks of special- interest groups that were trying to buy their votes. The fresh fire had changed the way business was being done in Washington. The people on the left were realizing their ideology was not right. The left knew it was going to have to get right or get left. Some of the public were outraged as they started working on stopping entitlements. In some places there were riots in the street.

In the early part of 2008, there were Federal Emergency Management Agency (FEMA) camps erected around the United States. There were three in Arkansas. I believe the government of the United States knew something was about to happen. These camps had razor wire on the inside of their fences, similar to prison camps. Look up FEMA camps on the Internet, and you will see what I am talking about. Police forces are now being trained by the military as well. If there is a big riot, like the one in Missouri, it will look like they were prepared for war. Before the church is taken up, it will get rough.

twenty-nine

Channing and Ellen:
This Is the Calm Before...

The waves of the ocean slapped back and forth as Channing and Ellen sat on the sand at the water's edge. They felt the grains of sand change formation with every wave around their hands and feet. The water covered Ellen's hand as they soaked in the ocean and the presence of God. Ellen and Channing both knew change was coming, and they were soaking up the anointing for battle. Ellen had always wanted a normal and quiet life without all the chaos, and so had Channing. Wherever there is sin unchecked, there is chaos, insanity, and a loss of direction. Channing said they might have to wait until the battle is over and they are in heaven to have the peace they want. Ellen nodded her head in agreement. Channing and Ellen did not like a fight. However, we have all done things that we did not want to do when we were fighting for a greater cause.

God's angels were all around them, guarding them and keeping them in all their ways. They also knew about and felt a coming battle. The feeling of anointing for battle was so heavy upon them that they felt shields around them and felt stronger in the spirit than they had ever felt. They were more guarded in their words because they knew in an instant it would come to pass.

"Peter started saying to Him, 'Behold, we have yielded up and abandoned everything once and for all and joined you as your disciples, sided with your party and accompanied you' (walking the same road you walked). Jesus said, 'Truly I tell you, there is no one that has given up and left house, or brothers or sisters or mother or fathers or children or lands for my sake and for the gospel's who will not receive a hundred times as much now and at this time—houses and brothers and sisters and mothers and children and lands, with persecutions—and in the age to come eternal life'" (Mark 10:28–30).

In John 15 Jesus talked of the parable of the vine and the branches. Any vine that did not bear fruit, the Lord would cut, which represents you and me. When this process of sanctification (being made into His image, which is sometimes painful) was done in his disciples (followers), they could then be trusted with more power. In verse 14 Jesus said we are his friends if we keep on doing the things that "I command you to do." In verse 15, Jesus says, "I do not call you servants (slaves) any longer, for thee servant does not know what the master is doing (or working out). But I have called you friends, because I have made known to you everything that I have heard from my Father (I have revealed to you everything that I have learned from Him). Verse 16 says, "You have not chosen me, but I have chosen you and appointed you that you might bear fruit and keep on bearing. So that whatever you ask the Father in my name He may give it to you."

After we have gone through the process, we get the power because He knows we are trustworthy. Shortly following, there is a transfer from follower to friend, and it is at that point that we can ask anything in Jesus's name, and it will be done by the Father in heaven.

Channing and Ellen and the rest of the believers that responded to the fresh fire from heaven obviously showed a friendship to God. Appearing out of the fresh fire were believers who were an army of God that could not be defeated because the believers could be trusted with the power of having what they say in Jesus's name. To be called a friend of God is a compliment and endowment that only few have known before now. There was a time of great tribulation coming. The friends of

God could feel it in their bones, and the angelic forces were everywhere, just waiting for a believer to speak the Word of God so the angelic forces could move.

thirty

You Could Tell People
Had Been Changed Instantly

The largest challenge that Congress had was to turn around the debt of the country. There were sharp cuts in Medicare and in social programs that made many people very angry. The UN peacekeepers had to be called out in many areas.

The United States owed China so much money that when they cut the check, they had to print enough money to take the dollar to a worth of less than twenty-five cents. They had no choice because China had recalled their loan.

What they did not know was Japan was right behind them. If they paid back foreign debt, a loaf of bread would cost twenty dollars. Something had to happen, or America, as well as the rest of the world, would be bankrupt.

The United States opened more factories and tried to be less dependent on foreign products. They voted out the North American Free Trade Agreement and started looking at gross national products and gross international products as a regulator to how much duty was charged on foreign products, like they used to do after World War II. It was a good time to do this in America because the people's money was not worth much anyway. It made us think about the past, when our focus was more on money than morality. This felt, smelled, and looked like judgment on sin, or "borrow now and pay later." They both are in the same pot, like peas and carrots.

China and the other countries in the world were very angry about NAFTA being removed. For years we had been their biggest customer. They thought for sure that under international law they were going to be able to take us over because we were not going to be able to pay back the debt. They had even increased their military because they knew we would not give it up easily, and Russia was going to be their ally.

When people started talking about a new world order, one world government, and one world religion, I knew something was up. Add one world economy governed by a select few, such as the G-20 summit. No one talked about who was going to rule. Some countries thought the G-20 group would step up to the plate, but not without a fight.

There have been more wars over money and religion because you have to be passionate about what you are fighting for. In America in recent years, we would accept name-calling, some terrorism, even the bombing of our embassies. However, if you mess with the stability of our economy, we will be at your doorstep in twenty-four hours.

thirty-one

Homeland Security or Riot Control

In the name of homeland security, our nation's police departments and special forces looked like the military. They had full-tinted face masks so we could not tell who they were. The UN peacekeepers wore blue outfits, and we saw their military vehicles on the road and at riots, raids, and protests. They had not tried to disarm America yet.

The riots came because people had become so dependent on the government that they were mad about having to get a job because the jobs were not coming back until more factories opened. Get people mad and fearful about their future, and we have the ingredients for a riot.

The FEMA camps were filling with people whothat would not be controlled by the new rules, and there was unrest everywhere. Not just in the United States—in other countries the economies were failing, and it was even worse. People were desperate, and desperate people do desperate things.

The people who did not repent when the fresh fire hit surely were not going to repent now. In fact, they were saying things like, "Where is your God now?" They were angry and bitter at God because who else were they going to blame when they would not look at themselves?

The free countries' governments were talking about their security, and the Communist countries' governments were talking about theirs. War was on every country's mind. However, it was then as if everyone became stealth, and they were not talking anymore. There was such an eerie silence, it was deafening and made us think something was about to happen—and it was.

thirty-two

The Antichrist

He had been groomed since birth for this position by the Illuminati, or the enlightened ones. You see, he was born in Rome, his mother died at birth, and no one knew who his father was. He had a supernatural charm about him. Everyone liked him, and his gift was getting people to get along by his use of witchcraft and manipulations. Some even called him the peacemaker. He had never had time for marriage. He said he was not given to women; his focus was on himself. He would laugh at himself and call himself a narcissist. At times he felt he had a God complex. He was jealous of God's position. He hid it well. He was not a religious man at all; however, he could play the part and was so educated in religion by the enlightened ones that he could play every role. He hated Christianity the most because his hatred for the Jews was infamous. He was a master of deception who supernaturally knew every language in the world fluently. His secret plan one day was to inherit the earth. He believed a totalitarian government was the way that life worked best, as long as he was in control. He was everything evil manifested in the flesh. I wondered if he was Satan's spawn.

All over the world we heard about him. His favor was unbelievable. Everything he touched seemed to work out. He fooled everyone except the believers in Jesus Christ. He was on their list of possible people who had the spirit of the Antichrist. The spirit of the Antichrist has been at work since the resurrection of Jesus Christ.

"And every spirit, which does not acknowledge and confess that Jesus Christ has come in the flesh (but would annul, sever, destroy, or disunite Him) is not of God (does not proceed from Him). This (no confession) is the spirit of the Anti-Christ, (of) which you heard of was coming, and now is already in the world" (I John 4:3).

thirty-three

Growing Hostilities between Countries

Growing trouble and hostility on the planet was coming to a head. All the countries of the world had stopped talking. Russia had aligned with Iran and all the other Middle Eastern countries against the Jews in Israel. China, Japan, and North Korea were forming an alliance against the United States, England, and our allies. The communist countries had bought land in Mexico and South America to put nuclear weapons in. You could feel the tension in the air. If mankind did not restrain itself, there could be a World War III. This had all been fueled by poverty, hand delivered by man's carnality of wanting everything now and instant gratification, and demanding ownership of it. I remembered what Satan said earlier at the G-20 summit. He said that the lust of the flesh, lust of the eyes, and the pride of life gets them every time.

Satan and his workers were busy from their underground vantage point down the street next to the Dome of the Rock. They could see the temple mound where announcements were being made about the first animal sacrifice in the new temple. They would be sacrificing a red heifer in the name of world peace. A prophet and a world dignitary, not yet announced, would have the honor of hosting the first sacrifice since the destruction of the temple. Israel was on high alert because of the threats made to the Jews. It was on every satellite broad-casting station in the world. Every eye beheld this event. Everyone who was anyone in man's eye talked about it.

thirty-four

Going Up?

It was a gorgeous fall day in Bismarck. The air was crisp, and the skies were clear. Channing and Ellen decided to have lunch at an afternoon gathering in their home. It seemed like everyone wanted to come. Channing asked Ellen who was coming.

Ellen said, "The list keeps growing, and I am glad it is a potluck." She said that Albert and Kim were coming, along with Rick and Carla, Pat and Ricky, Anna V. and her family, and of course Mark and Sheila, with both sides of their family.

There were picnic tables everywhere and a food table that never seemed to end. About forty people came to the gathering, and it was around four o'clock when Channing made the announcement to come into their great room and watch the first animal sacrifice in the new Temple Mount in Jerusalem. No one wanted to miss it, and it was the focal point on every news station.

It was dark in Jerusalem as the service began. The service was spoken in ancient Hebrew, so no one could understand the words. They announced a prophet we had never heard of and a man from Rome would have the honor of sacrificing the red heifer. Announcers talked about the history of the event, and all that we remembered was the coming down of the knife on the red heifer.

The whole room was full as we watched the event. And as soon as that knife went down, the walls of the room disappeared, and we were in a large open space in another dimension.

We would have been afraid, but our loved ones surrounded us. Ellen shouted out, "This is heaven!" and everyone began to worship.

Soon there were billions of people standing around the throne saying, "Worthy is the lamb that was slain from the foundations of the earth." The countenance on each face could not be expressed as the Lord Jesus Christ rose above the crowd. As always we felt as only our Father could make us feel, so enamored with the love that He had for each one of us. There were billions of people, and each felt that he or she had been with the Father and had some one-on-one time. It felt like liquid love and acceptance without a trace of guilt, shame, or unworthiness like we had felt on earth. Already the memories of the pain that we had suffered on earth had been taken away because He was the balm of Gilead that soothed and removed any memories of the separation that sin had brought us. It was naturally supernatural. Some of our ancestors that we had never met were there, and we were all rejoicing together. The worship went on for a very long time but without the feeling of time passing for we were in eternity now. We were busy seeing the place the Lord Jesus Christ had prepared for us with urgency because the master said there was much to learn and relearn. We all had to be in one accord to fight the future battle.

thirty-five

The Antichrist Revealed

"When they saw the appalling sacrilege (the Antichrist and the false prophet making an atonement for the sins of the world when Jesus Christ was the only acceptable sacrifice to God; it was called the abomination that astonishes and makes desolate) spoken by the prophet Daniel, standing in the holy place—let them take notice, ponder and consider this. Then let those that are in Judea flee to the mountains. Let him who is on the housetop, not come down and go into the house to take anything. And let Him who is in the field not turn back to get his overcoat. And alas for women who are pregnant and those who have nursing babies in those days! Pray that your flight may not be in the winter or on the Sabbath. For then there will be great tribulation (affliction, distress, and oppression) such as has not been from the beginning of the world until now—no, and never will be again" (Matt. 24:15–21AMP).

All of this happened as the Antichrist came down with the knife because he was Satan's son offering a holy sacrifice, defiling the temple.

Shortly after the sacrifice, there were lying wonders (which is Satan's imitation for miracles) shown that were supposed to be a confirmation that in reality the Antichristhe was the coming messiah. As he spoke, people of all religions waited on a coming prophet or messiah, and they took his message like bait. He was a master deceiver.

thirty-six

Immediate Chaos

As soon as the Antichrist came down with the knife, there was a change in the audio and video on the television broadcast because of a loss of employees. Millions of people on the planet disappeared in the blink of an eye. Transmitters went down, planes came down, and utilities were interrupted by the loss of personnel. All of the televisions and radios switched to public service announcements because of the magnitude of what had just happened and the loss that had not been calculated. Unmanned vehicles of every description and type were empty, without a trace of the church of Jesus Christ.

The church was gone and with them was an absence of stability, restraint, comfort, and peace. Some people committed suicide as they looked for their loved ones, only to find out that they were gone. They had heard of this happening but had always blamed it on their families wanting to force their belief system down their throats. There was regret and remorse by some, and others realized what had just happened. They repented and asked the Lord to forgive them, and He did. Oddly enough, for some a distant stare came over their faces as they went into survival mode, as if this had never happened, because long ago the god of this world had blinded their eyes from seeing the glorious Gospel and receiving salvation.

thirty-seven

The False Prophet Endorses the Antichrist

The Antichrist was in rare form as he supernaturally brought up the transmitters and repeaters all over the world. Satellites were knocked out of orbit as the earth rocked like a drunkard, because when the graves flew open, the earth gave up the dead in Christ. The seas did also. The pressure and then release was so strong, it shook the very foundations of the earth. When his voice and image appeared on the screen, all the translators were off-line; however, everyone heard him speaking in their own dialect. This was one of his first lying wonders (false miracles).

His mood was animated and energized by the chaos and drama that had riddled the planet with confusion. He fed on the stories as they came in. He wrote the book on confusion and deception, so he was now in his element.

He thought this was his moment and nothing could take it away from him.

A prophet from the world council of churches stepped up to the platform. This man represented a one-world religion that anyone could follow without threatening any government social system because they did not believe in sin anymore. He offered salvation without turning away from anything. We could be whoever we wanted to be and do any act we wanted because God made us that way. Without hesitation, he turned to the man of sin on the platform with him and made the announcement that the Antichrist was in fact God manifested in the flesh, and the crowd went wild.: "Here is the one god who is anything that you want him to be." We could be any religion and hear what we needed to hear to believe that he was the promised one, the savior of the world.

thirty-eight

If It Feels Good, Do It

With a proud look and a false appearance of humility, he spoke. "The current disappearance of people on the earth is by far the most shocking event. For years and years we have been hindered by Christianity. The doctrine they represented was presented at first by a virgin birth, of all things, and then a savior that at best was only a prophet. Jesus teaches turning away from your natural desires and following Him. I tell you to follow your own impulses that I give you and follow what comes naturally."

With that, the party started. Even in the face of the most suffering that the planet had ever seen, he preached, and a false sense of security and peace hit the crowd. His anointing felt like a form of lust instead of holy power. The crowd began to drink the wine of his fornication and began to worship him as God.

The false prophet said that a few weeks ago, when the heat signature was so strong from outer space, our government went to red alert. He said that his friends in the universe finally came and got the Christian's and took them away.

All the governments of the world trusted him and began to move quickly to a new world order with the Antichrist in control. When he met any confrontation or rebellion to his ideas, he took their lives. His followers said that he killed wonderfully. His goal was to be the totalitarian ruler of the world; apathy and passivity were going to let it happen. With him leading, his plan was to take them to a time of tribulation such as the world had never known or ever would know.

Satan and all of his minions watched with joy and anticipation from their vantage point down the street. Satan said that he had never felt like he was in control of mankind until now, and, boy, did he have a score to settle. He knew the next time he would see the Lord Jesus Christ would be when the Lord Jesus Christ himself stood on the Mount of Olives to usher in the Battle of Armageddon.

thirty-nine

It's All about Jesus

There was worship like I never thought existed on earth. All of our ancestors from the beginning of time were worshiping the way they used to, and we were worshiping our way. It came out of our mouths as worship of the Lord Jesus Christ. Jesus Christ taught classes every day on what it meant to live in heaven, and soon we would be assigned jobs because he had a lot going on. We had no problem with our memories anymore. Our bodies and minds became glorified the second we crossed over. The retention level was supernatural, and all the talents we had were only enhanced for use in worship and the jobs we were assigned. We would certainly do the Lord's work and love every second of it.

The beauty of the throne room took our breath away. I had never seen on earth the beasts that were around the throne. The attention to detail was perfect and in order and done out of love for the master. He was still the talk of heaven. The angels in heaven were just as amazed with us as we were with them. Some of them looked like walking battleships but, at the same time, operated in the love of God.

Although the judgment seat of Christ had not taken place yet, I could tell that the least of us on earth were the greatest here. The deeds the angels of God talked about the most were the deeds done when no one was looking.

There were angels coming from and going to earth to support some 144,000 Jewish evangelists called to win over the lost in the first three and a half years of the tribulation period. There were people who came to know the Lord because of the disappearance of the church. They knew that aliens had not taken the church away. They had relatives and loved ones who had warned them of this happening, and they had no one to blame but themselves. They were going to have a hard way to go now because Christians would soon be hunted like game for the Antichrist put a bounty on their heads.

forty

Christians Will Be Hunted like Game

Reba and Brent came from Christian homes and had two boys who were fourteen and eighteen who were left behind as well. The whole family had been to church a few times, and Rebas mother seemed to smother them with her religion. They did not make time for church. They found it boring because they had never been born again. They were left behind, and at first they were angry. Now they felt it was their own fault for not allowing the Holy Spirit to draw them and for pushing the spirit away every time because they feared what it might require. That was behind them now because they had repented, asked the Lord to come into their lives, and changed.

The streets were still jammed with unmanned cars and wrecks because the freeways had not been cleared. There was no food in the grocery stores, so they went to their Rhebas mothers house. Long ago she had started preparing for an event like this and wrote them a letter about what to do. They headed through the back roads to her house to read the letter and see what possible resources they could use. When they got to her house, it was the way she had left it. There was a generator still running on natural gas or propane. The lights and freezers were still working. Reba ran toward the letter behind the wooden matchbox holder next to the kitchen stove, right in the place where Rhebas mother said it would be.

Dearest Loved Ones,

By the time you see this letter, I will be in heaven. I tried with all my heart to convince you of the urgency of change and submission to the Word. I prayed for you every night and hope by now you have made a change and can follow this plan. I love every one of you and will do what I can. There is a six-month supply of food among the rations in the storage building, freezers, and cabinets. The generator will run until the tank goes dry. I hope this gets you by until the streets clear. Whatever you do, don't take any markings from the government— a mark or chip. They will tell you that you cannot buy or sell without it. Barter or trade for your services with other believers. I have left you seeds to plant your own garden. There are chickens in the chicken house, and the old well house has a manual pump on it. If you are found out, the Antichrist and his bunch will kill you. I just pray you can avoid the plagues at the three-and-a-half-year mark. Please do not blame God for the suffering that you will have to go through because it cannot be compared to the glories in heaven.

Again, I love you with all my heart, and I tried to prepare for you as much as I could afford.

Your loving mother,

Margaret

Reba could not catch her breath because she was crying so hard. The others cried as well and rubbed Reba's back, saying it was going to be OK, even though they knew it would not. One good thing about the family was that they knew how to hunt and farm and would not be taken out without a fight.

Because of the suffering that would be taking place for the next seven years, the days were going to be the hardest the planet had ever seen. The number of fellow believers was scarce.

forty-one

Satan Is a Negatively Charged Pawn

Long ago, the Father created negative and positive forces. Electricity moves from positive to negative. The planet runs on two magnetic poles; one pole is negative and one positive. It will be the negative things in our lives that push us to the positive. If we refuse to flow with the direction of the current, we can short the system by trying to go against God's design. If we embrace the process and let the negative push us to the arms of Jesus and repent, the process is faster and less painful.

Because of his fall from heaven, the devil has been the negative force. At one time or another, like pawns being pushed to our destinies, the Holy Spirit was drawing us, and the devil was pushing us, and some still rebel. The negative things in our lives (our needs) have pushed us to the positive (the Lord). The people who were left behind refused to take Jesus Christ as their Lord and escaped the punishment of the tribulation period. Jesus Christ is the only sacrifice for sin that God accepts.

One of the many reasons Jesus Christ came to earth was to understand sin's allurement. No one had ever tempted Him. It was not good enough for him to just give us some laws. He wanted to be our kinsman redeemer. He came to find out what it was like to be us, tempted and tried in every area of life, and then, being completely innocent, He took our sins and bore them in His own body. He did that so we might love him enough to want to find out what it felt like to be Him. Unless we suffer with Him or for His cause, we will never reign with Him. We all have had to make stands for our faith—some more than others. We have had to suffer with new believers until Christ be formed in them. Or we may have had to suffer without reason, and still I say that we will not know what it is like to be Jesus until we have fellowshipped in His sufferings.

As the tribulation period goes on, the suffering will increase in strength. The negative forces will make us name our weaknesses (it will cause them to surface) to the point of a positive or negative conversion. For the first forty-two months, there will be some true conversions, and then people will become harder and harder. They will curse God with every event. These are the people who are made for hell's prison.

forty-two

What's Next?

I have a very limited knowledge of this period of time because I have never felt that I would go through it. I am going to have to rely on the Word to tell you what will happen so you can envision the first three and a half years of the tribulation period yourself. Following the tribulation period, there is another three and a half years called the Great Tribulation, a period such as the world has never known.

"Then I saw as the lamb broke one of the seven seals, and as if in a voice of thunder I heard one of the four living creatures call out, 'Come!' And I looked, and the rider carried a bow. And a crown was given to Him, and he rode forth conquering and to conquer" (Rev. 6:1–2).

This is a picture of the Antichrist because he came forth to conquer. (This could not be the Lord Jesus because he already conquered.)

The second seal is found in Revelations 6:3–4. "And when He broke the second seal, I heard the second living creature call out, 'Come!' And another horse came out, flaming red. And its rider was empowered to take peace from the earth. So that men slaughtered one another: and he was given a huge sword."

This is a picture of the Antichrist's rise to power and the resistance he faces by anyone who tries to stop him. Unfortunately, a lot of new converts are killed for their faith in the Lord Jesus Christ.

Revelations 6:5–6 reads, "When He broke open the third seal; I heard the third living creature call out, 'Come and look!' And I saw and beheld a black horse, and in his hand the rider had a pair of scales (a balance). And I heard what seemed to be a voice from the midst of the four living creatures, saying, 'A quart of wheat for a denarius (a whole day's wages) and three quarts of barley for a denarius: but do not harm the oil and the wine.'"

This famine was caused by the earth's response to the Antichrist and the first seal. His quest was to balance the power in his direction because at this junction he was controlling the masses with food.

Revelations 6:7 states, "And when He had opened the fourth seal: I heard the fourth beast, come and see. And I looked and beheld a pale horse black and blue (as if made so by bruising) and the name of the rider was Death, and Hades (the realm of the dead) followed him closely. And they were given authority and power over a fourth part of the earth to kill with the sword, famine, plague (pestilence, disease), and with the wild beast of the earth."

Death and hades are on a rampage because of the first three seals.

They know their time is growing shorter.

"When the Lamb broke open the fifth seal, I saw at the foot of the altar the souls of those whose lives had been sacrificed for (adhering to) the word of God and the testimony they had borne. They cried with a loud voice 'O (Sovereign) Lord, holy and true, how long now will it be that you will sit in judgment and avenge our blood upon those who dwell upon the earth?' Then they were each given a long, flowing, and festive white robe and told to rest patiently a little while longer, until the number should be complete of their fellow servants and their brethren who were to be killed as they themselves had been" (Rev. 6:9–11).

This was the cry of the martyrs of the first three and a half years of the tribulation period.

"When He (the lamb) broke open the sixth seal, I looked, and there was a great earthquake; and the sun grew black as sackcloth of hair (the full diskof), the moon became like blood. And the stars of the sky started dropping to the earth like a fig tree shedding its unripe fruit out of season when shaken by a strong wind. And the sky rolled up like a scroll and vanished, and every mountain and island was dislodged from its place. Then the kings of the earth and their noblemen and their magnates and their military chiefs and the strong and (everyone, whether) slave or free hid themselves in the caves and among the rocks of the mountains. And they called to the mountains and rock, 'Fall on (before) us and hide us from the face of Him Who sits upon the throne and from the deep-seated indignation and wrath of the lamb.' For the great day of His wrath (vengeance, retribution, and indignation) has come and who is able to stand before it?" (Rev. 6:12–17) AMP.

From what I understand and have been taught, this marks the three-and-a-half-year mark when anyone who made a stand for God has been killed by the Antichrist's army, and God starts pouring tribulation on the earth such as the world has never seen. The 144,000 Jewish evangelists have been taken off the earth by the Lord. The ones left are the wicked and evil even in the face of all that has been done, will not believe and repent.

forty-three
Reba, Brent, and Their Boys

Reba and Brent had prayer meetings in different places every night as the small group of believers in the area pulled together. They cooperated their gardens together so they did not starve and hid their food away from the unbelievers. They lived their lives in fear because of the decisions they made before the church was taken up.

Reba went into town to see if she could find anything she needed and ran into a prayer partner on the court square.

They talked about what had been going on in their lives, and as believers we know that Jesus's name is always brought up. They were excited about their newfound faith, and Reba talked about the difference it had made in the lives of Brent and the boys. They were both rejoicing, and the UN peacekeepers, who were now under control of the Antichrist, heard the conversation. Six UN peacekeepers in A blue Hummer marked with the UN logo killed them, cut their heads off, and left their bodies on the court square four days.

When Brent and the boys found out, they went on a UN-peacekeeper hunt and killed several of them. However, they were so outnumbered that they were finally killed, all at the same time, because they would not deny their faith in the Lord Jesus Christ.

They died an honorable death, which may have gone unnoticed on Earthearth. There was a party in heaven when their souls united with their families. What more could they ask for? For what lies ahead for the unbelievers on the planet is tribulation such as the world has never seen.

It was an unseen blessing that it happened when it did.

forty-four
The 144,000 Jewish Evangelists

Revelations 7:1-4 reads AMP, After this I saw four angels stationed at the four corners of the earth, firmly holding back the four winds of the earth so that no wind should blow on the earth or tree or sea or upon any tree. Then I saw a second angel coming up from the east (the rising of the sun) and carrying the seal of the living God. And with a loud voice he called out to the four angels who had been given power to injure the earth and the sea. Saying, 'Harm neither the earth nor the sea nor the trees until we have sealed the bond servants of our God upon their foreheads.' And then I heard how many were sealed (marked) out of every tribe of the sons of Israel: There were 144,000 (12,000 from each tribe)."

From the teaching I received growing up, these were Jewish bond servants or evangelists who could not be affected by the great tribulation but were sent here to preach in the midst of the chaos. Then there is another group that was innumerable, wearing white robes, which had washed their own garments. In Revelations 7:14 one of the elders asked, "Who are these people clothed in white?"

The reply was: "These are they that have come out of great tribulation (persecution) and have washed their robes and made them white in the blood of the lamb." The martyrs like Reba and her family. If you will read to the end of the chapter, I was amazed that Jesus put a tabernacle over them and offered to shepherd them and wipe all tears from their eyes. What a forgiving and merciful God we serve. This all took place at the three-and-half-year mark of the tribulation period.

forty-five
Seven Resurrections

When I was seventeen, I heard a sermon that has stuck with me ever since. When the evangelist was asked about the rapture of the church, he said that word is not mentioned. The words "caught up" and "resurrected" were. He believed there were seven resurrections mentioned in the Bible. I believe this as well. He said there was Enoch, Elijah, and Jesus. Then he said there will be the church that is resurrected before the Antichrist is revealed, Then the 144,000 Jewish Marked Bond servants will be resurrected In Revelation 7:1-4. Following that ressurection is the apperaing of all the martyrs in Revelation 7:14 and finally the two witnesses, who we will read about in a minute, will be caught up. I have heard different teachings, but when I go back to allowing the straight word to reveal itself, this is what I come back to. When I say "straight word," I believe Jesus would not hide anything that the common man who was seeking the truth could not understand the basics as well as a theologian. Some go into more detail, but this is Revelations 101. Now, let's get back to the Great Tribulation such as the earth has never seen.

forty-six

Seven Bad Trumpets of Judgment

"When He (the lamb) broke open the seventh seal there was silence for about an hour and a half in heaven (while the angels prepared for the trumpet judgment). Then I saw the seven angels that stand before God and to them were given seven trumpets. And another angel came and stood over the altar. He had a golden censer, and he was given very much incense (fragrant spices and gum which exhale perfume when burned), that he might mingle it with the prayers of all the people of God (the saints) upon the golden altar before the throne. And the smoke of the incense (the perfume) arose in the presence of God (the saints), from the hand of the angel. So the angel took the censor and filled it with the fire from the altar and cast it upon the earth. Then followed peals and thunder and loud rumblings and blasts and noises, and flashes of lightning and an earthquake. Then the seven angels that had the seven trumpets began to sound them. The first angel blew his trumpet and there was a storm of hail and fire mingled with blood cast upon the earth. And a third part of the earth was burnt up and a third part of the trees were burnt up and all the green grass was burnt up. The second angel blew his trumpet and something resembling a great mountain, blazing with fire, was hurled into the sea. And a third of the sea was turned to blood, a third of the creatures living in the sea perished, and a third of the ships were destroyed. Then a third angel blew his trumpet, and a huge star fell from heaven burning like a torch and it dropped on a third of the rivers and the springs of water. And the name of the star is wormwood. A third part of the water was changed into wormwood, and many people died from using the water, because it had become bitter. Then the fourth angel blew his trumpet, and a third of the sun was smitten, and a third of the moon and a third of the stars, so that the light for a third of them was darkened, and a third of the daylight itself was withdrawn, and likewise a third of the light from the night was kept from shinning. Then I looked and I saw a solitary eagle flying in mid-heaven, and as it flew I heard it crying with a loud voice, Woe, woe, woe to those who dwell on the earth, because of the rest of the trumpet blasts which the three angels are about to sound" (Rev. 8:1–13) Amp.

"Then the fifth angel blew his trumpet, and I saw a star that had fallen from the sky to the earth; and to this angel was given the key to the shaft of the abyss (the bottomless pit). He opened the shaft to the abyss (the bottomless pit), and the smoke like the smoke of a huge furnace puffed out of the long shaft, so that the sun and the atmosphere were darkened by the smoke from the long shaft. Then out of the smoke, locusts came forth on the earth, and such power was granted them as the powers of the earth's scorpions have. They were told not to injure the herbage of the earth, nor any green thing, nor any tree, but only to attack such human beings that do not have the mark of God (the 144,000 Jewish evangelists) on their forehead. They were not permitted to kill them, but to torment (distress and vex) them for five months, and the pain caused them was like the torture of a scorpion when it stings a person. And in those days people will seek death and not find it; and they will yearn to die, but death evades and flees from them. The locusts resembled horses equipped for battle. On their heads was something like golden crowns. Their faces resembled the faces of people. They had the hair of women, and their teeth were like lions' teeth. Their breastplates (scales) resembled breastplates made of iron, and the (whirring) noise made by their wings was like the roar of a vast number of horse-drawn chariots going at full speed into battle. They have tails like scorpions, and they have stings, and in their tails lies their ability to hurt men for the five months. Over them as king they have the angel of the abyss (the bottomless pit). In Hebrew his name is Abaddon (destruction), but in Greek he is called Apollyon (destroyer). The first woe or calamity has passed; behold two others are to follow. The sixth angel blew his trumpet, and from the four horns of the golden altar which stands before God I heard a solitary voice saying to the sixth angel that had the trumpet, "'Liberate the four angels who are bound at the great river Euphrates.'" So the four angels who had been in readiness for that hour in the appointed day, month, and year were liberated to destroy a third of mankind. The number of their troops of cavalry was twice ten thousand times ten thousand (200,000,000); I heard their number was. And in my vision the horses and their riders appeared to me like this: the riders wore breastplates the color of fiery red and sapphire blue and sulfur or brimstone yellow. The heads of the horses looked like lions' heads, and from their mouths poured fire, brimstone, smoke, and sulfur brimstone. A third of mankind was killed by these three plagues—by the fire, smoke, and sulfur brimstone that poured from the mouth of the horses. For the power of the horses to do harm is in their mouth and also in their tails. Their tails are like serpents, for they have heads, and it is by means of them that they wound people. And the rest of humanity that were not killed by these plagues even then did not repent of the worship of the works of their own hands, so as to cease paying homage to the demons and the idols of gold, silver, bronze, stone, and wood, that cannot hear, see, or move (idolatry). And they did not repent of their murders or their practice of magic (sorcery, drug abuses) or sexual vices or thefts" (Rev. 9:1–21 AMP).

forty-seven

The Judgments Still
Do Not Break Their Will

Before we go any further in the book of Revelations, I feel the need to tell you that Revelations 1:1 simply says, "This whole book is a revelation of Jesus Christ unveiling His divine mysteries."

Although a lot of people think these judgments are symbolic, they are not. John is telling you what he saw just like He saw it. The plagues of Egypt were just as they were written.

I used to think that the book was so full of judgment that I could not stand to read it. Now I see it as Jesus being so willing to forgive when God's conditions are met. His conditions are that Jesus Christ is the only sacrifice for sin that is acceptable to God. It also shows me that in a world where there are no absolutes, God still absolutely hates sin, and if we refuse the sacrifice that He so mercifully provided and refuse to turn from our wicked ways and repent, there remains no sacrifice for sin. The people left from here on out are the most hardened, willful group of people who have ever been. In my opinion, they have put themselves in this position (as you and I did). As we will see later, in the face of angelic activity, demonic activity, vials of wrath, and plagues, they still do not examine themselves and say, "Could it be me who is in the need of a savior? Could I have brought this on myself? Do I need to ask God to forgive me and stop doing the sin that I am operating in?" No. They curse God instead. They are unto themselves an idol.

When the martyrs landed in heaven and Jesus offered to shepherd them and wiped the tears from their eyes, I thought, "Amazing grace, how sweet the sound that saved a wretch like me." I fell in love with Jesus even more because He is so quick to forgive and forget. Oh, how I love Jesus.

forty-eight

The Two WitnessesHE TWO WITNESSES
(Possibly Enoch and Elijah)

"A reed (as a measuring rod) was given to me, shaped like a staff, and I was told, 'Rise up and measure the sanctuary of God and the altar of incense and number those who worship there. But leave out your measuring the court outside the sanctuary of God; omit that, for it is given over to the gentiles (the nations), and they will trample the holy city underfoot for forty-two months, or three and a half years.' And I will grant the power of prophecy for 1,260 days, or three and a half years, dressed in sackcloth. These witnesses are the two olive trees and the two lamps stands, which stand before the Lord of the earth. And if anyone attempts to injure them, fire pours out of their mouth and consumes their enemies; if anyone attempts to harm them, thus he is doomed to be slain. These two witnesses have the power to shut up the sky, so that no rain shall fall during the days of their prophesying or their predictions of events relating to Christ's kingdom and its speedy triumph; and they also have the power to turn the water into blood and to smite and scourge the earth with all manners of plagues as often as they choose. But when they have finished their testimony and their evidence is all in, the beast (monster) comes out of the abyss or bottomless pit and will wage war on them, and conquer them and kill them and their dead bodies will lie exposed in the open street in a public square of the great city, which is in a spiritual sense called, by the mystical and allegorical name of Sodom and Egypt, where also their Lord was crucified. For three and a half days men from all races, tribes, languages, and nations will gaze at their dead bodies and will not allow them to be put into a tomb and those on the earth will gloat and exult over them and rejoice exceedingly, taking their ease and sending presents in congratulations to one another, because these two prophets had such a vexation, trouble, and torment to all the dwellers of the earth. But after three and a half days, by God's gift the breath of life again entered into them and they rose up on their feet, and great dread and terror fell on them that watched them. Then the two witnesses heard a strong voice from heaven calling to them, 'Come up here!' And before the very eyes of their enemies they ascended into heaven in a cloud and at that very hour there was a tremendous earthquake and one tenth of the city was destroyed or fell; seven thousand people perished in the earthquake, and those that remained were filled with dread and terror and were awestruck, and they glorified the God of heaven. The second woe has passed, now the third woe is speedily to come. The seventh angel blew his trumpet, and there were mighty voices in heaven shouting, 'The dominion, kingdom, and sovereign rule of the world has now come into the possession and become the kingdom of our Lord and of His Christ the messiah, and he shall reign forever and ever for the eternities of eternities. The earth is now returned from Satan to its rightful owner hand, The Lord Jesus Christ'". (Rev. 11:1–15 AMP).

forty-nine

Heaven Prepares for Battle

Ellen, Channing, and the group from Bismarck were not seg-regated by denomination at all. They knew each other, and there was a common interest in heaven and Earthearth in these times of great tribulation. Heaven was alive with all kinds of angels and beings that who were made for warfare. For train-ing purposes, the billions of people were able to watch and see the warfare tactics. Everyone's spiritual senses were height-ened the moment they he or she arrived in heaven. They were using 100 percent of their brains, which came in handy when the Lord Jesus Christ got up to teach. He was so full of love and mercy and slow to anger when his conditions were met. Ellen said that she was still floored that the two witnesses were killed and laid on Golgotha, the same place our Lord was crucified. At this time, there was still salvation experienced on Earthearth, happening since the mark of the beast had come out. This was the number and name of the beast, indelibly written on every head as a prerequisite to buy or sell. Once they took this mark, they sold out, and were doomed to hell, and the very counte-nance of their faces would change to the rebellion and lack of self-control that had brought them there. What a shame for the people, when all they had to do was repent for their sins, ask the Lord Jesus Christ to come into their lives, be saved, and turn away from their wicked ways.

Ellen said that she had never felt such peace and well-being in any place before. Family was very important to the Father, so we were not separated from our family. We were more in love with our family than ever because our differences were gone, and the works of the flesh left with them. Our home outside the city was the most beautiful place I had ever seen. Animals' tongues had been loosened, and they talked like the rest of us. Everyone had their beloved pets from earth as well as any other pets that they wanted. The plants were more alive, and the colors were vivid. The grass never got too tall, and weeds were not seen. The plants and rocks talked. The smells were clean and crisp every day. Nothing compared to the glory and brightness of the Father. His brightness was the light source in heaven. And everything done there was about and through our love for Him.

The teaching from the Lord Jesus Christ put everything together from all the denominations, and everyone had a job to do. Jesus was never idle, so heaven was a busy place with lots of things going on.

He made heaven a lot like earth, except for the city itself. The size of the city was fifteen hundred cubic miles, and it had twelve foundations named after the twelve apostles made of twelve precious stones, and it sat on the planet. There is more that I will share with you later. We are at the three-and-a-half-year mark in the tribulation period where there is tribulation such as the world has never known.

fifty
The Last Three and a Half Years

The next three and a half years are full of symbolism and imagery that is difficult to explain with a clear heart, so I will take you through what I do understand; using an outline provided by Dake Annoitated Bible in the post- rapture events section.

In Revelations 12:7–12AMP, the announcement was made that the earth was back in the hands of the Lord. Lucifer became god of this world when he took it from Adam and Eve in the garden. However, God will not take possession of it until Jesus lands on the Mount of Olives at the battle of Armageddon.

Because the earth is the Lord's, there will be a battle in the heavens. Satan will alter his form to a red dragon and fight the sun-clothed women. When he is defeated there, he will move to God's remnants on earth, making them martyrs. A beast out of the sea will be given the power to rule over those nations. The false prophet then begins worshiping the beast. The 144,000 Jewish evangelists that had been marked with the seal of God will be resurrected to heaven.

The scene moves to heaven, where an angel will announce the fall of Babylon and the doom of the beast worshipers. Vials will be prepared and poured out on the earth's still-unrepentant occupants. Keep in mind that angels will fly around, preaching the gospel, all the battles that the earth has seen and will see with their own eyes. The unrepentant will have to believe in God, just like the devils do, and tremble. Vials will be poured on the earth to judge the sin, and in my opinion, this will be

God's last attempt to pressure them to repent and turn fro m their wicked ways.

"The first vial is poured and creates grievous sores on mankind" (Rev. 16:2-1).

"The second vial is poured out and turns all of the seas to blood.

The third vial is poured out and turns the rivers to blood. The fourth vial is poured out and great heat becomes present. The fifth vial is poured out and darkness is everywhere. The sixth vial and the great river Euphrates is dried up. Then three unclean spirits come out of the dried-up Euphrates river and attempt to assemble an army from the nations of the earth" (Rev. 16:13–16).

"Then the seventh vial is poured out and Babylon and other cities are destroyed" (Rev. 16:17–21).

"Then there is warfare announced on the Lamb of God" (Rev. 17:14).

"The marriage supper of the lamb" (Rev. 19:1–10).

"The second advent of Christ on the earth, when he lands on the Mount of Olives and fights with the saints at the Battle of Armageddon" (Rev. 19:19–21).

"The binding of Satan for 1000 years" (Rev. 20:1–3).

"This will start the one-thousand-year reign of Christ in heaven" (Rev. 14:6).

fifty-one
The Marriage Supper of the Lamb

Ellen and Channing had a family reunion bigger than all outdoors.

The animals and grandchildren kept everyone entertained while the glory of God was seen and felt for miles from the throne room. In the forefront of everyone's minds was their first love—-Jesus. It was exactly what Jesus had hoped for from the beginning—us loving Him, and Him loving us, because we wanted to. The table went for miles upon miles, but they felt so close to Jesus that it was as if they were right next to Him.

And for a moment, if only in my mind, the earth again is without form and void, and darkness is upon the face of the deep, and in the underworld there lies the devil and all of the army of hell, just like there was in Genesis 1:2 before the spirit of God moved over the face of the waters. The earth is a dark planet with prison cells, which were reserved for the doomed and the damned waiting for the white- throne judgment, where the evil ones are judged for what they did and left undone, each according to his or her deeds.

The End for Now

www.ingramcontent.com/pod-product-compliance
Lightning Source LLC
Chambersburg PA
CBHW071132090426
42736CB00012B/2103